Healing racial trauma

A PRACTICAL GUIDE TO HEALING THE
SHAME, ANXIETY, FEAR, AND TACTICS IN
ORDER TO DEVELOP FREEDOM

Bethany Key

Copyright - 2020 -

All rights reserved.

The content contained within this book may not be reproduced, duplicated or transmitted without direct written permission from the author or the publisher.

Under no circumstances will any blame or legal responsibility be held against the publisher, or author, for any damages, reparation, or monetary loss due to the information contained within this book. Either directly or indirectly.

Legal Notice:

This book is copyright protected. This book is only for personal use. You cannot amend, distribute, sell, use, quote or paraphrase any part, or the content within this book, without the consent of the author or publisher.

Disclaimer Notice:

Please note the information contained within this document is for educational and entertainment purposes only. All effort has been executed to present accurate, up to date, and reliable, complete information. No warranties of any kind are declared or implied. Readers acknowledge that the author is not engaging in the rendering of legal, financial, medical or professional advice. The content within this book has been derived from various sources. Please consult a licensed professional before attempting any techniques outlined in this book.

By reading this document, the reader agrees that under no circumstances is the author responsible for any losses, direct or indirect, which are incurred as a result of the use of information contained within this document, including, but not limited to, - errors, omissions, or inaccuracies.

TABLE OF CONTENTS

	INTRODUCTION	5
CHAPTER - 1	FEELINGS OF SHAME, GUILT, AND ANXIETY	9
CHAPTER - 2	FORMS OF RACIAL TRAUMA	17
CHAPTER - 3	TYPES OF RACISM	21
CHAPTER - 4	KEYS TO EDUCATION AGAINST RACIAL TRAUMA	31
CHAPTER - 5	LEARNING FROM THE HISTORY OF RACIAL TRAUMA	35
CHAPTER - 6	UNDERSTANDING YOUR RACIAL-ETHNIC IDENTITY	45
CHAPTER - 7	FOOTPRINTS AND SYMPTOMS OF RACIAL TRAUMA -PHYSIOLOGICAL CHANGES	51
CHAPTER - 8	STEPPING INTO FREEDOM-IDENTIFY	61
CHAPTER - 9	HOW TO SUPPORT YOUR OWN HEALING?	67
CHAPTER - 10	CONTRIBUTING FACTORS TO ETHNICITY AND RACIAL TRAUMA	75

TABLE OF CONTENTS

CHAPTER - 11
HOW TO STOMP OUT RACIAL
TRAUMA   79

CHAPTER - 12
CAUSES AND EFFECTS OF RACIAL
TRAUMA   91

CHAPTER - 13
IDENTIFYING THE PROBLEM   99

CHAPTER - 14
WHAT IS ANTI-RACIAL TRAUMA?   111

CHAPTER - 15
SOLIDARITY AGAINST RACIAL
TRAUMA   117

CHAPTER - 16
HYPOCRISY WITHIN US   127

CHAPTER - 17
RACIAL TRAUMA THEORIES IN THE
MODERN AGE   135

CHAPTER - 18
WHAT IS SOCIAL JUSTICE?   145

CHAPTER - 19
FIGHTING RACIAL TRAUMA   153

CONCLUSION   159

INTRODUCTION

We will meet a few people of color along the way and read their stories of oppression, healing, and resilience. How many of you presently live with the poisonous plagues or perilous pitfalls of complex racial trauma? Are you still shrinking in the shadows of shame and sin from childhood or adolescent racial traumas? Have you experienced physical, psychological, emotional, and/or sexual abuse and terror over the course of your lifetime or within the past several years (or even decades)? Has the loss of a loved one catapulted you into the complex claws of racial trauma, a precarious path without a mindful map, or any concrete escape plan as it involves numerous intersections, roadblocks, and potholes on our minds, bodies, and spirits daily?

1. How brainwashing has been used to control the mind

Brainwashing is a type of psyche control that objectives an individual's capacity to settle on decisions without being forced or pressured.

2. Inferiority complex and racial trauma

In America, bigotry is normal and comes in different structures and shapes including police ruthlessness and racial profiling among others. This has brought about low confidence among the minority particularly blacks. As a matter of fact, low confidence is the main purpose behind inclusion in lawful offenses. Why? Since bigotry is about genuine force and when one individual is denied their capacity, they will respond to show their disappointment.

3. Superiority complex psychology

It is both absurd and ludicrous to realize that the prevalence complex is a type of guard system which individuals utilize to reward for the substandard complex. Such individuals accept that their worth is relied upon demeaning and harming others.

4. Assassinating a person's character with racial trauma

The brain science of prejudice includes character death

Character death can be portrayed as a planned and steady procedure that expects to insult or chaos up with the validity of an individual or gathering of individuals. Individuals who kill others' characters utilize different strategies including misdirecting data, demeaning, slander, and control. This may prompt dismissal by other people who may not have the foggiest idea about the genuine truth—does this ring a bell? Prejudice is incredible and will frequently retaliate through character death.

Nothing is outlandish

On the off chance that today we are living in very much assembled houses and not caverns, if today we are utilizing current ovens and not kindling, if today we are strolling completely dressed and not exposed, nothing is unimaginable. At some point—bigotry will be history.

Unlike treating a broken bone with a cast, the path to healing from racial trauma is one that can take dangerous detours and boisterous bumps on the road to recovery and resilience (literally!). Tan's quote about wounds is so valid and applicable to the visible and invisible ones that impacted my body, mind, and soul. Are you even conscious of your wounds from complex racial trauma? Did you endure or witness atrocious acts of domestic violence or intense scenes of intimate partner violence (IPV) when dating, married, or while growing up in a dysfunctional household or volatile situation? Are you currently still harboring woes and wounds beyond words from service in the military, exposure to war and violence as a former refugee or immigrant, or endured atrocious acts of rape, molestation, incest, or sexual assault? This will offer you some light amid the darkness that you have had to deal with for far too long.

CHAPTER - 1
FEELINGS OF SHAME, GUILT, AND ANXIETY

As a result of exploring life, love, and learning beyond labels in as far as what complex racial trauma is and its typical sources, we will present you with some relevant research, practical examples, and beneficial exercises to the understanding complex racial trauma's overlapping, revolving, and devastating physical, psychological, spiritual, socioemotional, sexual, behavioral, financial, and vocational ramifications. Our ability to rise above this diagnosis depends on our capacity to navigate all these complicated effects and manifestations, so channel the lyrics to "Eye of the Tiger," "Rise Up," or "Roar" "We Are The Champions," or whatever pumps you up to defy complex racial trauma.

Reverting back to the title of and the revolving doors' metaphor, how many of you feel automatic panic, fear, or just plain annoyance when entering revolving doors in any office building, tourist attraction, or hotel? I personally dislike the feeling of entering them as other people are also pushing simultaneously and following me so closely. It probably reflects the feelings and realizations that I do not have control, something that my racial trauma has caused me to struggle with most for most of my adult life.

How do people with complex racial trauma struggle with control issues? In my own case, whether I was trying to regulate my weight, grades, perceptions from others, achievements at work, I always felt like I had to be the best, so I was super competitive at work, in school, and with my peers. I also was highly distrusting and suspicious of everyone and everything. I never felt safe.

Are you competitive, aloof, depressed, or anxious? I suffered from high anxiety as well as hyper-competitiveness. My inflated sense of ego also greatly hindered my relationship dynamics that caused me to be overly bossy, super controlling, and extremely suspicious of everyone and everything. Do any of these tendencies presently reflect your own struggles with complex racial trauma as far as managing the physical, psychological, spiritual, socioemotional, sexual, behavioral, financial, and vocational ramifications?

Put down the mops, toss aside the dustpans, and sideline the sweeper for this one. As you complete this essential exercise, think of your own life in terms of a house, dorm, or apartment metaphor. In order to be sane, happy, and healthy, we must clean each room equitably and live in each area for balance, right? Well, this mindful technique urges us to take an inventory of how complex racial trauma manifests in our own lives or "houses" before we do a clean "sweep" to purge the dust from the past. Answer honestly about any areas that warrant you to spring clean the racial trauma dust and cobwebs from the critical facets of your life and wellbeing holistically:

- Physical dirt.
- Psychological grime.
- Spiritual dust bunnies.

Additionally, it is important to clarify that DNA is not different between blacks and whites, in fact, it is almost exactly the same by far, what cannot be denied is that there are genetic variations but only within the African continent there is more genetic variety than in the whole rest of the world, a fact that has demonstrated that life started there and from there it spread to the whole planet. As a last important fact, there is no visual characteristic that allows us to differentiate the genetic similarities or differences in us, so classifying someone as white, brown, or black is an absurdity that expresses nothing more than the simple color of the skin.

Aware of the equality between all classes and colors, great movements have been created in order to assert the universal rights of human beings in the face of all kinds of contempt, movements led by men who are willing to give their own lives for that cause. There have been very important and renowned figures whose efforts came to make a considerable difference, although these worthy representatives have been key players in each victory obtained are not responsible for one hundred percent of them, there is a larger group of anonymous heroes who in silence and discipline have managed to create liberating enterprises, deserving greater credit although they are only satisfied with receiving the benefit of rights respected for them and theirs, but it is inevitable and regrettable reality, there is still much to be done.

Activism is necessary to gain new grounds and not lose those already won, let us remember that thanks to the constant and firm fight against discrimination and racial violence, it was possible to eradicate the separation and privileges in the use of public transport, alliances were created between multiple races in all sectors affected by poverty and hit by supremacist elitism, with this the well-known campaign of the poor obtained the law that allows the right to vote. A highly accentuated criticism in the middle of marches for the resources destined to senseless wars in Vietnam, same that would have a greater benefit if they were used in programs of aid to the poor, that mobilization was the one that originated the law of service of immigration and nationality. The agitation in the streets in defense of the universal guarantees of each individual, as long as it is persistent and under the slogan of non-violence, will generate firm and sustained results as it has happened in the past, we must raise our voices unanimously without lowering our arms but without generating regrettable disturbances that threaten the integrity of public goods. The tactic of the state security forces will always be to use violence and aggression to disperse the concentrations, let them be the violent ones without falling into their provocations because that is the bait they will use to destroy us, but when we raise our voices telling the truth but calmly our pleas will be heard in the right instances and sooner or later justice will come knocking at our door.

Men and women with extraordinary potential have been victims of a millennial sabotage that keeps them away from uncertainty but imprisons them and makes them smaller, destroys their character and decimates their will, preventing the large-scale development of self-realization and freedom of thought, action and time. Those responsible for this sabotage are already clearly identified and are known as the morality of conformity, the acceptance of facts as irrefutable divine predestination, and self-commiseration.

All human beings should constantly ask and question themselves because certain issues are considered attractively desirable and others extremely repulsive, who does not become a sheep unaware of the morality implanted by the media as right and wrong, this sheep accepts as absolute reality any fact, rumor, news or dubious affirmation because of the simple lack of own criteria because we have been educated from the first infantile schools to the most important university institutes that to question the teachers and the established precepts is something amoral and disrespectful, nevertheless, in that way we are suggested to accept everything without any type of claim that turns us to the convenience of a few in simple automatons within a system devised against us.

The most atrocious truths are hidden from the incredulous and passive gaze of public opinion, between information and disinformation a battle is led that seeks to subject each individual with strong pressure until he becomes so tiny and ridiculous that he only aspires to cover his most basic needs without any intention of standing out, that is to lose self-respect.

Who is at the top of the social food chain considers himself as the man who dictates the steps that society should take, the image of himself is that of a god incarnate with a supposed moral superiority to the rest and the others for him are just a flock that must obey his whims without any excuse. Paradoxically the majority behaves like that flock, only a few behave like free-thinking individuals capable of undertaking their own path, an idealism free of unfounded thoughts and a human character capable of benefiting many in their steps.

I raise my voice in these words when I ask myself about the whereabouts of the leaders who want to be part of a new generation of free from the oppressive chains of any supremacist system and build a society in which the color of your skin does not matter and your origins are not an impediment but neither are they a guarantee before the cultural environment, a community in which you can and must earn by your own merit access to better opportunities. What I propose is that no one should be despised but neither should things be put on a silver platter so easily that no one can appreciate the satisfaction of effort and sacrifice.

CHAPTER - 2
FORMS OF RACIAL TRAUMA

Racial trauma is real

There are various ways that people of color experience racial trauma: as stated below. This is the reality of people of color from generation to generation. We are a trauma bond and we carry this from our ancestors into the modern world. This has left us inadequate and inconstant pursue of self believe. We project our insecurities to others in society, all this because of a system that has left us at a disadvantage. We have been lead to believe we are less superior and we need guidance from the white man.

Transgenerational Racial trauma

The trauma across the family is called transgenerational racial trauma. We may be prone to certain individual attitudes or actions are modeled in our families or community.

We ask ourselves questions such as: Who am I?

Personal Racial Trauma

My family experienced personal racial trauma as we get to call each other names from the slave trade era. Names such as "nigga" that is a form of us personalizing such names as a form of copping. This is seen in hip-hop culture, yes it is a way of identity but also as a coping mechanism, we find power in empowering such words and not allowing the white people to call us back. We may thing this us empowering ourselves but it is a way of trauma coping passed down generation to generation.

Physical Trauma

This happens when one is physically beaten due to your beliefs. Such treatment has been ongoing and has led to the creation of hate groups that still exist in the modern-day, this has created fear in people of color as we feel oppressed and cannot speak out in case of injustice. In the modern era, politicians have taken advantage and use such groups to inflict pain on people of color knowing the public will blame us.

Vicarious Trauma

Vicarious trauma occurs when we hear of detailed trauma stories or watch of survivors of racial abuse i.e. on T.V, newspaper such stories cause us to relate and bring past fears to reality. TV has managed to make such stories to look as we people of color are the ones on the wrong. This not only creates fear in us but the general public. We have seen situations where white people take advantage of this, they treat us as outcasts and use the police as a shield knowing very well if this was covered by news outlets they will get an advantage.

Microaggressions

Microaggression comes in the form of slights or messages communicated verbally or nonverbally. i.e. when we are cursed of being over sensitive thus stereotyped this can hinder our personal life as we believe we are prone to react, and at the same time, other races overlook us in professions that require a calm sense of self. In modern-day people of color will earn less than a white person in the same position due to this as the employee sees us as volatile thus we cannot handle all that is required of the given profession.

CHAPTER - 3
TYPES OF RACISM

We can speak of structural racial trauma, which is something that is, in some way, attached to the structures of our society. This is the mildest form of racial trauma and difficult to perceive, and therefore somewhat dangerous. We can identify as symptoms of this form of racial trauma the fact that black people win, according to statistics from the 2016 IBGE census, less than white people. We also found a lower level of education among the black population.

In our daily lives, we use racist expressions, often without realizing it, and the verification of these actions and situations combined with the belief in normality can be the factor of greatest risk for society when talking about racial trauma. Expressions of language and racist terms reinforce structural racial trauma (so strongly rooted) and allow discrimination to permeate all means, persecuting victims everywhere, as language is capable of entering any sphere of human life. Therefore, it is not a question of being "politically correct," but of recognizing that there is someone who is offended by certain expressions because he suffers in his skin the negative consequences of the discrimination that originated them.

A Typology of Racist Acts

A better understanding of the dimensions that structure the relationships between perpetrators and victims is a necessary stage to define the possibilities of the reaction of people who are the object of racial trauma to violence or discrimination experienced. The analysis of the different cases related to the 0800 SOS Racial trauma led us to distinguish two particularly important dimensions that define the relationship between the perpetrators and the victims: power and level of organization.

The power exercised over the victims can be of two types: certain authors are in a position of formal power vis-à-vis the victims: they have the possibility of exerting a direct influence on their living conditions, either because they apply the laws (which may be discriminatory or applied unfairly) or because they control access to social or economic assets that they exclude, without respecting equity, victims of access to them. Other authors have only informal power: they have the will to discriminate, but they do not have the means of coercion against the victims; it is true that they can threaten them, they can have weapons or other means of intimidation, but they do not represent the law, nor do they exercise a hierarchical social function over them.

The other dimension is the level of organization of the aggressors: Racist acts can emanate from people who are part of an institution, an organization or a group with a more or less elaborate racist ideology; in this case, the authors act as members of an organization that perceives racial trauma (or at least certain manifestations of racial trauma) as normal behavior. Racial trauma can also be the expression of disorganized individuals who act violently or discriminatory on their own initiative, according to personal a priori, related to collective prejudices, but in an unstructured manner. When they adopt racist behaviors, they know more or less consciously that they are in contradiction with the norms of equality that prevail in society.

The combination of these two dimensions allowed us to develop a typology in which we can distinguish four forms of racial trauma: interpersonal racial trauma, racial trauma for abuse of function, institutional racial trauma, and doctrinal racial trauma.

The typology we present here was built on the basis of a continuous process of interaction between empirical data and theorizing work. It is a production work of what Glaser and Strauss (1966) call a grounded theory. The raw material on which we base ourselves is the stories of racist discrimination or violence, such as were presented to the anti-racist telephone number. The calls received indicate that for the complainant, the racist act lived or observed, exceeds the limits of what is tolerable. We then work with a material that touches on racist behavior considered as visible by those affected. We do not directly address the field of latent racial trauma, prejudice, structural discrimination.

Institutional Racism

We define institutional racial trauma as that which is exercised by an organization, often the state, that holds back the power to claim "the monopoly of legitimate physical violence" (Weber, 1959) and to define legality. In this case, racial trauma, which most often takes the form of discrimination, responds to a legal norm that does not respect the principle of equal treatment. It is then the law or the general policy of the institution that is discriminatory. This is particularly the case for immigration rules based on "cultural criteria": for example, immigrants originating from a Third World country or from Eastern Europe do not in principle have the right to obtain a work and stay permit in Switzerland (or in the countries of the European Union) because they do not have a good color passport. Sometimes, other laws, such as those related to Social Security, may be discriminatory towards immigrants based on the type of stay authorization they have or their national origin. 25% of the reported cases correspond to this type of racial trauma. This type of discrimination has been analyzed by authors such as Radtke (1990) and Bukow (1992). From their perspective, it is the practices, discourses, and institutional norms that contribute to producing discrimination against minorities. In the Swiss case, Weill Lévy and Grünberg. (1997) have shown that the discourse and practices in question were elaborated at the beginning of the century by the "foreigner police," created in that period. This contributed to propagating an ideology of the "Überfremdung," which considers foreigners as a threat to national cohesion since their presence "excessively alters the Swiss population" 1. Other authors have also mentioned that immigration policy, by dividing the world into different circles, for the recruitment of immigrant workers, creates a hierarchy based on cultural difference. By acting in this way, it designates certain human beings as radically different. And "threatening," thus laying the groundwork to justify keeping them at a distance from the space controlled by the State of arrival, through discriminatory treatment (Caloz Tschopp, 1993; Goldberg, 1998). An example of this process is what we have defined as the criminalization of immigrants by immigration policies. In fact, the means of fighting against what has been called "illegal migration" form the basis of the mechanisms of their persistence and reproduction. In other words, anti-clandestine policies produce and maintain clandestinity (Bolzman, 1998).

These are mainly discriminations that take an administrative form: it is the refusal to grant, renew, or transform a stay authorization or the threat of not doing so. At the bottom, the central issue in this type of situation is the right to stay in the country of arrival. But there are also other discriminations that concern social insurance, access to training, or other public benefits. Often this type of situation is not considered racist. It is perceived as normal that a foreigner, especially if he is from a Third World country, is the subject of arbitrary decisions that do not need to be made explicit. Furthermore, it should be noted that many acts of this type reflect a narrow legal system that places affected people in impossible human situations.

In certain cases, institutional racial trauma (particularly the issue of permits) allows a third party to exercise violence in all impunity in the private sphere against the person concerned. The perpetrator of violence knows in effect that he runs little risk of being denounced by his victim, who is in a position of weakness due to his precarious status. This is the case, for example, of conjugal violence. The spouse who has the nationality of the country of residence or a stable permit is allowed to exercise permanent blackmail towards the victim because they know that the right of stay of the victim depends on the marriage.

Interpersonal Racism

In this case, racial trauma is the result of the action of individuals or informal groups that do not have a structured power over the victims, nor do they claim a strong racist ideology to act violently or exercise discriminatory behavior towards them. It is "ordinary" racial trauma where the authors transform an interpersonal conflict into a racist act, attributing to the attacked biological, ethnic, or cultural characteristics that make cohabitation with him impossible and legitimize violent or discriminatory actions against him. 38% of calls concern this type of racial trauma[3]. This type of behavior is close to what Vieworka (1998) defines as cultural or identity racial trauma. Different complementary reasons can explain this type of behavior. This can be attributed to authors who channel their discontent with their living conditions through the mechanism of the "scapegoat" (Girard, 1972), who protest against the problems they encounter in everyday life by imputing them to "foreigners" (Oechste and Zoll, 1985), who feel threatened by an incomprehensible and uncontrollable world represented by the Other (Bell, 1964). They may also be people who have lived through authoritarian socialization (Adorno et al., 1950), who are intolerant of ambiguous situations (Frenkel Brunswik, 1949) or who have imbued themselves with a xenophobic ethos. Another explanation refers to racial trauma used as strategic conduct: certain people can, in a conflict situation.

Interpersonal violence can reach different levels of intensity, it is often expressed through verbal aggressions' (in two-thirds of situations of interpersonal racial trauma, the victims complain of having received insults, insults, threats), but also through behaviors of segregation (avoidance of all physical contact, use of the same objects, frequenting the same places, rejection of any "mix," etc.), as well as, to a lesser extent, through forms of harassment (anonymous phone calls, noise, and other behaviors aimed at making the victim's life unbearable) and through physical assault. These different forms of aggression are often personalized; that is, they are aimed at precise victims and have strong emotional content.

Doctrinal Racism

In its most extreme version, doctrinal racial trauma is exercised by individuals or groups who do not have formal power, but who act on the basis of a racist ideology inspired by the speeches of far-right organizations with which the authors sympathize. This racial trauma is directed more consciously and strategically against specific categories of victims, with the aim of creating and maintaining a climate of prejudice and discrimination against them. 16% of the cases analyzed correspond to this type. This type of behavior corresponds to the classic analyzes of extreme right organizations. This is related to what Taguieff (1997) has defined as racial trauma ideology. They insist on irreducible differences with respect to those who are defined as others and hide those that exist within their own group or deny what is common to different groups.

Mixed Racism

The distinctions between the four forms of racist acts mentioned are analytical. In reality, sometimes different shapes mix and even reinforce each other. In fact, in 14% of the cases, we have verified the existence of racist behavior "in cascades," where, to first discrimination or aggression, others are added in which new authors intervene. For example, the situation of a person who is harassed by a neighbor, who is supported by the custodian of the property in their conduct. The victim complains to the police who give the attackers reason, without having listened to her.

CHAPTER - 4
KEYS TO EDUCATION AGAINST RACIAL TRAUMA

But is that always synonymous with understanding? What can we do as parents so that our children escape racist attitudes?

In general, in humans, there is a tendency to be afraid of something new or different. It is an instinctive reaction, which does not occur in the same way in all people and, in most cases, is a protection against ignorance. Thus, the first way to avoid racist attitudes is to show children diversity and difference as something natural and enriching.

Keep in mind that in this case, the moral discourse (what is right and what is wrong) is going to be insufficient. It must be accompanied by an intellectual reflection (within the possibilities according to the age of your child), explaining the reasons why all human beings are equal and that as such, we must live with the formula of respect and tolerance.

How do Children Learn Racial Prejudice?

From an early age, children already learn about racial differences and prejudices from their referents, their parents, relatives, teachers, etc.

The process of learning racial prejudice does not differ much from the process of learning a new language. At six months of age, a baby's brain can already recognize racial differences. Between the ages of 2 and 4, children can internalize racial biases. And at 12 years old, many children have already established their beliefs, which makes it more difficult to reduce their racial prejudices and improve their cultural understanding.

Education for Diversity

As parents, we can act in different key aspects so that children get used to diversity and thus avoid racist comments or attitudes towards people of other beliefs, cultures, or countries. If these factors are present in your education, racist-type reactions will greatly decrease.

Be a good example

Identify and correct your own comments and actions that may foster racial prejudice.

It fosters friendship with people from other countries

Relationship with other people is the most natural way of understanding difference. This is applicable both if the child has classmates from other countries and if the parents have friends who favor this exchange.

It stimulates the learning of other languages

A new language provides a new way of seeing and understanding the world.

It teaches music, tales, gastronomy and traditions from other places

In this way, the little ones will see the difference as something playful and fun. Since traveling, or reading stories, playing with apps or learning to cook recipes from other countries are good ways to teach other customs and ways to understand diversity.

Talk to children about racial trauma

Communication is fundamental for two things: that they understand what attitudes can be considered as racist or as stereotypes without justification. There are endless ways to stimulate a conversation about racial trauma: movies, television, travel, or even consulting a world map or an Atlas together.

It is important to note that in many cases, children will find children of immigrants in class, who have come for various reasons, some of them out of necessity. Understanding this can make peers help them in their integration process, especially in the case of adolescents.

According to a study promoted by the Ministry of Labor and Social Affairs, there are still many attitudes of discrimination in the classroom, by some young people who use racist insults to offend their colleagues from abroad.

However, the same study also concludes that these same attitudes increasingly provoke more rejection among adolescents who do not adopt them. In addition, in the conclusions, it was observed that the influence of the family is decisive in the attitude of the students.

Remember that to create an inclusive culture, we all have to recognize and reflect on our own racial prejudices so that we can change our attitude towards those who are unfair or who may cause harm to other people.

CHAPTER - 5
LEARNING FROM THE HISTORY OF RACIAL TRAUMA

The civil rights term refers to the freedom of citizens to live equally in society. The American Civil Rights Movement of the 1950s and 1960s refers to the combined efforts of people throughout the United States who organized protests, voter registration drives, and other community events with the purpose of ending legal discrimination against Black people. While often peaceful, many of these efforts turned violent due to harsh retaliation by government agents, police, and White people who wanted to preserve the status quo by keeping intact segregation and systemic racial trauma.

Systemic, or institutional, racial trauma is an established system of laws, policies, and practices that deprive one group of resources while protecting and providing those resources for the group in power. Civil disobedience, or acts of peaceful rebellion against unjust laws, in which citizens engaged to dismantle systemic racial trauma and inequality, was one of the most effective methods of resistance at this time.

The Civil Rights Movement specifically addressed the race and skin-color based laws that were designed to discriminate and separate. Since the practices that infringed upon the rights of Black Americans were legal, the American Civil Rights Movement sought to overturn these laws and give Black Americans the same inalienable rights as White Americans.

The Fight to End Slavery

Civil rights for Black people in the United States has been an issue of debate since our founders declared independence from Great Britain in 1776.

Slavery, the practice in which one group of human beings is owned as property and forced into servitude by another, has long divided the country. Because enslaved people were considered chattel, or property, many White people believed Black people were not entitled to the same rights that they held, and therefore accepted the institution of slavery. This argument was dependent on the unfounded bias of skin color that stemmed from the Judeo-Christian misinterpretation of the Curse of Canaan, also known as the Curse of Ham. The story goes that Ham, the father of the Canaan people, witnessed his father Noah's drunkenness and did not look away. In anger, Noah cursed Ham to a life of servitude. Clearly, the issue of slavery was one in which religion and politics were dangerously intertwined, despite America being founded as a place of religious freedom and decreed by our founders to be a country in which the government would remain untainted by religion. The legal practice of slavery divided the country and continued to do so despite being abolished by the 13th Amendment.

The 13th Amendment

Deeply held religious beliefs, coupled with politics, can create quite a divide. When Thomas Jefferson, who himself was a slave owner, wrote early drafts of the Declaration of Independence, he spoke out against the horrors of the slave trade, but not against slavery itself. However, the Continental Congress chose not to include any mention of slavery or the slave trade in the final draft of the document, as they believed that, because African people were bought and sold, they were personal property and the government could not tell its citizens what to do with their property.

Both the British and the Colonists' Armies recruited escaped and enslaved African men to fight in the American Revolution. It was common practice to promise them freedom, which they would receive when the war was won. Most enslaved people who fought did not, in fact, receive their freedom, and the fight to abolish slavery continued. In fact, some of the earliest civil rights leaders were abolitionists who were active in the fight against slavery.

Of course, abolishing slavery was just the beginning of the fight for civil rights. Once Congress ratified the 13th Amendment in 1865, as well as the 14th Amendment in 1868, Black people were granted citizenship as natural-born Americans. On paper, this meant that they now had all the rights given to White people, and Black men now had the right to vote. Yet it would take more than a hundred years for the federal government to uphold the rights that they had given on paper to people of color.

Important Abolitionists and Activists

Frederick Douglass

1818-1895 -Douglass, who escaped slavery, became one of the leading abolitionists of his time. His autobiography, which he revised and republished three times, made him extremely popular but also made him the target of recapture attempts. He traveled the world speaking about the evils of slavery and worked with Elizabeth Stanton to promote women's suffrage. He was also the first Black American nominated for Vice President of the United States.

Booker T. Washington

1856-1915 -An enslaved man who was emancipated, Booker T. Washington became one of the most influential leaders of Black liberation. He believed that former slaves should focus more on vocational studies and community building, and less on attempts to fight segregation. He became the first president of Tuskegee University and helped to form the National Negro League. In 1895, Booker T. Washington and other Black leaders struck a deal with southern White leaders. This agreement was never written down or formally recorded. In it, Booker T. Washington and others agreed that Black people in the South would submit to segregation, not ask for the right to vote, nor retaliate against racial violence or try to end discrimination. In return, they would receive a free basic vocational education (mechanics, teaching, nursing, etc.) W. E. B. Du Bois named it the Atlanta Compromise.

Nat Turner

1800-1831 -Born into slavery, Nat Turner led one of the bloodiest revolts against slavery in the United States. He believed that he was chosen by God to fight evil. He led a group of 50 slaves who traveled to different plantations and killed White slave owners, women, and children. His rebellion caused harsher laws against southern abolitionists but also garnered the support of northerners who believed that slavery was wrong.

Harriet Tubman

1822-1913 -An enslaved woman who escaped captivity and went on to lead the Underground Railroad. She helped to free 700 enslaved people and served as the first woman to lead an armed expedition during the Civil War.

W.E.B. Du Bois

1868-1963 -A social justice activist, Du Bois helped found the NAACP. He was the first Black American to receive a Ph.D. from Harvard University. Du Bois fought against racial trauma and discrimination in education and employment. He actively spoke out against lynching and Jim Crow laws. He also fought against the idea of the genetic superiority of the White race, writing numerous dissenting essays and articles. His collection of essays The

Souls of Black Folks serves as an example of the great intellect and humanity of Black people. Although he believed in equality for all, he did not speak out in favor of women's voting rights because the leaders of the Woman Suffrage Movement did not actively and publicly support Black rights. Du Bois was against the Atlanta Compromise, believing that Black people should fight for equality and rights.

The South After the Civil War (Reconstruction)

Jim Crow laws, named for a minstrel routine that degraded Black Americans, consisted of any legislation that served to keep segregation intact. These laws, many passed in 1870, required that Blacks and Whites remain separated on public transportation, in parks, cemeteries, schools, and theaters. There were separate water fountains, and Black people were often forced to enter buildings through the back door, also known as the servants' entrance. Additionally, there were laws that made interracial marriage illegal. The goal was to prevent interaction between races and to continue the notion that the races were not equal.

Yet her decision to no longer accept the humiliation of segregation laws sparked the Montgomery Bus Boycott, with Dr. Martin Luther King Jr. as its spokesperson. Although

Rosa Park's arrest was the catalyst for the boycott, its roots can be traced back to a letter written by The Women's Political Council (WPC), a group of Black women who were civil rights activists and who were already planning a boycott of the Montgomery bus system.

The purpose of the Montgomery Bus Boycott was not to repeal segregation laws, but rather to force the city to hire more Black bus drivers. Its organizers also sought to change the seating policy to one that allowed seats to be filled on a first-come-first-served basis, and to demand to be treated with respect and courtesy. Their case, Browder v Gayle (1956) was used by the Supreme Court to end segregation on buses. The Supreme Court's ruling increased the momentum of the American Civil Rights Movement.

"People always say that I didn't give up my seat because I was tired, but that isn't true. I was not tired physically… No, the only tired I was, was tired of giving in."

Rosa Parks

It was not the first time that the Supreme Court had shot down state-sponsored segregation. The ruling in the case, Brown v Board of Education of Topeka (1954), which was argued by NAACP attorney Thurgood Marshall, had overturned segregation and declared that "separate but equal schools were inherently unequal." This decision struck down the ruling in Plessy v Ferguson (1896), which stated that if the facilities and services offered to Black Americans were equal to those offered to White Americans, segregation was legal. However, since many White people believed Black people were inferior, local governments often ignored the "equal" portion of Plessy's "separate but equal" ruling? The ruling in Brown v Board of Education forced states to integrate their public schools. Between this ruling and that of Browder v Gayle, desegregation was underway.

Dr. Martin Luther King Jr.'s unique ability to inspire the public with his speeches made him the face of the movement. His use of non-violent protests, which publicly shamed the very violent police and government officials who tried to suppress the movement, made him hugely popular among Christians. To that end, he was elected president of the newly-formed Southern Christian Leadership Conference (SCLC), where he continued to lead and preach about the power of love in moving the nation forward. However, much of the progress made by the movement was due to lesser-known activists and organizations.

CHAPTER - 6
UNDERSTANDING YOUR RACIAL-ETHNIC IDENTITY

It is the research of these differences in a safe, positive, and growing environment. It is about comprehending each other and moving further on simple tolerance to accepting and embracing the rich dimensions of diversity present within each person.

Diversity is a reality made by individuals and groups from a vast spectrum of demographic and philosophical dissimilarities.

"Diversity" means more than just accepting and tolerating differences. It is a set of conscious acts that involve:

Understanding and acknowledging the interdependence of culture, humanity, and the natural environment.

It is practicing mutual respect for attributes and experiences that are different from our own experience. It also refers to the understanding that diversity includes ways of being and also techniques of knowing;

The concept of diversity encompasses acceptance, embrace, and respect.

It means understanding that each individual is distinctive, and recognizing our individual differences

When the population differences are well represented within a community, it is cultural diversity. These include race, age, ability, language, ethnicity, nationality, socioeconomic status, sexual orientation, religion, or gender differences. The group is said to be diverse if a wide variety of groups are represented in it. Cultural diversity has become a hot-button issue when applied to the workplace.

However, we are typically seen by others in terms of one specific part of our identification, often with our life experiences and selves excluded. For creating more humane and supportive societies, recognizing and supporting the diversity which marks our modern relationships is an essential aspect.

The difference is a simple word with an apparently simple definition. But when we look deeper, it seems there is a whole world behind it.

They are different in the way they look, in how they speak, in what they eat. That's not all of it, but one part of the discussion.

We are different in the way we think: people have different opinions, thoughts, ideas, values, and beliefs that are tamed, for example, by politics, religion, education, and culture.

We are diverse in the way we talk. Think about how many dialects, languages, or accents you are aware of, not only in the world but within your own country. These ways of communicating include body language, sign language, and other forms of nonverbal and verbal communication. Examples of these include signaling with your hands or even the whole body, volume and pitch of the voice, speed of the statement, and so on.

We are diverse in our goals, dreams, backgrounds, and experiences, as well as in the way we experience sexuality, gender, and identity.

We are diverse in how we listen, learn, store, and interpret information—some people are better with images, some with swords, and others with music.

We are also different in opportunities that life throws at us. Consider the imbalance between people around the world in terms of access to quality food and water, education, healthcare, law, and employment opportunities, and proper living conditions. And this list can continue infinitely.

All of these aspects add to shaping our own distinctive and beautiful identities and influence the way we live and experience life and interact with our girdle.

The question arises here is then "why?" Why we have to think about Diversity when we are already working with peace education?

If we think about the broad meaning of Diversity, maybe we should be asking the question ourselves, "why not?"

By itself, diversity can have different meanings. The definition itself is in a diverse form. Implications range from a fact of being distinct or varied, to a variety of opinions. The essential point in the formal meaning is that it indicates there is a point of difference. There are several other areas.

Identity is concerned mainly with the question: "Who are you?" What does it mean to you? It relates to our fundamental values that define the choices we make (e.g., relationships, career). These choices tell us who we are and what we value. We can assume that the investment banker giver more value to money, while the college professor gives more importance to education and helping students. However, very few people choose their identities. Instead, they simply continue the values of their parents or the dominant cultures in a different form, fulfilled people are able to live a life that is true to their values and can pursue meaningful goals. Lack of a logical sense of identity will lead to uncertainty about what someone wants to do in his life.

A significant task of self-development during an early age is the differentiation of different selves as a function of social context (e.g., self with father, mother, close friends) with an awareness of the potential refutations.

Identity may be inherited indirectly from parents, friends, and other role models. Children come to explain themselves in terms of how they think their parents perceive them. If their parents think of them as worthless, they will start to think of themselves as ineffective. People who understand themselves as appreciated, remember more positive thoughts and comments than negative statements.

Psychologists argue that identity formation is a matter of "finding oneself" by matching one's potential and talents with available social roles. One of the most demanding selections a person ever makes is defining oneself within a social world. In the struggle of identity, many end up choosing darker characters, such as gambling, drug abuse, or compulsive shopping, as a compensatory way of experiencing aliveness or staying away from depression and meaninglessness.

CHAPTER - 7
FOOTPRINTS AND SYMPTOMS OF RACIAL TRAUMA -PHYSIOLOGICAL CHANGES

The general objective of ACT is to increment psychological flexibility—the capacity to contact the present minute all the more completely as a cognizant person and to change or persevere in conduct while doing so serves esteemed closures. Psychological flexibility is set up through six center ACT forms. Every one of these zones is conceptualized as a positive psychological attitude, not simply a strategy for staying away from psychopathology.

Acceptance

Acceptances educated as an option in contrast to experiential evasion. Acceptance includes the active and mindful grasp of those private occasions occasioned by one's history without superfluous endeavors to change their recurrence or structure, particularly while doing so would cause psychological damage. For instance, tension patients are educated to feel nervousness, as an inclination, completely and without protection; pains patients are given strategies that urge them to relinquish a battle with pains, etc. Acceptance (and diffusion) in the ACT isn't an end in itself. Or maybe acceptance is encouraged as a strategy for expanding esteems based action.

Cognitive Diffusion

Cognitive delusions strategies endeavor to change the unfortunate elements of contemplations and other private occasions, as opposed to attempting to adjust their structure, recurrence, or situational affectability. Said another way, ACT endeavors to change how one interacts with or identifies with contemplations by making settings in which their unhelpful capacities are lessened. There are scores of such strategies that have been produced for a wide assortment of clinical introductions. For instance, a negative idea could be observed impartially, rehashed for all to hear until its sound remains, or treated as a remotely watched occasion by giving it a shape, size, shading, speed, or structure. An individual could thank their brain for such an intriguing idea, name the way toward intuition ("I have the idea that I am nothing worth mentioning"), or look at the recorded contemplations, sentiments, and recollections that happen while they experience that idea. Such strategies endeavor to lessen the precise nature of the idea, debilitating the inclination to regard the idea as what it alludes to ("I am nothing worth mentioning") instead of what it is legitimately experienced to be (e.g., the idea "I am a whole lot of nothing"). The consequence of diffusion is generally decreased inauthenticity of, or connection to, private occasions as opposed to a quick change in their recurrence.

Being Present

It advances continuous non-critical contact with psychological and natural occasions as they happen. The objective is to have customers experience the world all the more legitimately, so their conduct is progressively adaptable, and in this way, their actions increasingly predictable with the qualities that they hold. This is cultivated by permitting usefulness to apply more authority over conduct; and by utilizing language more as a device to note and depict occasions, not just to foresee and pass judgment on them. A feeling of self-called "self as a procedure" is actively energized: the defused, non-critical progressing depiction of considerations, sentiments, and other private occasions.

Self-Context

This is a consequence of relational frames, for example, I versus You, Now versus then, and here versus There, human language prompts a feeling of self as a locus or point of view, and gives an extraordinary, profound side to ordinary verbal people. This thought was one of the seeds from which both the ACT and RFT developed, and there is currently developing proof of its significance to language capacities, for example, sympathy, theory of the brain, feeling of self, and such. In a word the thought is that "I" develops over huge arrangements of models of viewpoint taking relations, however since this feeling of self is a context for verbal knowing, not the substance of that knowing, it's cutoff points can't be deliberately known. Self as the context is significant to some degree because, from this point of view, one can understand one's progression of encounters without connection to them or an interest in which specific encounters happen: in this manner, diffusion and acceptance are cultivated. Self as the context is encouraged in the ACT by care activities, analogies, and experiential procedures.

Qualities or Values

Qualities or values are selected characteristics of purposive action that can never be seen as an object; however, it can be launched minute by minute. ACT utilizes an assortment of activities to enable a customer to pick life bearings in different spaces (for example family, vocation, otherworldliness) while undermining verbal procedures that may prompt decisions dependent on evasion, social consistency, or combination (for example "I should value X" or "A great individual would value Y" or "My mom needs me to value Z"). In ACT, acceptance, diffusion, being available, etc. are not finishes in themselves; instead, they make way for an increasingly fundamental, values, reliable life.

Committed Action

Finally, ACT energizes the improvement of more prominent and more significant examples of viable action connected to picked esteems. Right now, looks especially like conventional conduct treatment, and practically any typically cognizant conduct change strategy can be fitted into an ACT convention, including introduction, abilities obtaining, molding strategies, objective setting, and so forth. In contrast to values, which are continually launched, however, never accomplished as an article, solid objectives that value predicted can be achieved, and ACT conventions quite often include treatment work and schoolwork connected to short, medium, and long term conduct change objectives. Conduct change endeavors thus lead to contact with psychological obstructions that are tended to through other ACT forms (acceptance, diffusion, etc.)

How ACT Works

People are the main creature ready to make connections (relationships) among words and thoughts. For instance, we can relate apples and oranges to the general idea of natural products. While this is unfathomably valuable for preparing our general surroundings, it can make issues when we partner harmless thoughts in a negative example. After some time, individuals can start to relate ideas like disappointment or uselessness to themselves, setting them up for progressively negative results later on.

ACT works by instructing patients to recognize and proceed onward from these points of view, instead of permitting them to get imbued. While pessimistic considerations can be reasonable and proper reactions to specific circumstances, they don't characterize who an individual is as an individual, and ought not to keep that individual from proceeding onward with their life.

At the point when you see a specialist for the ACT, you'll start by figuring out how to tune in to how you converse with yourself, called self-talk. The principle center will be your self-talk encompassing awful mishaps and other harmful parts of your life, as undesirable connections, physical issues, and then some. Your specialist will, at that point, assist you with deciding if these perspectives are things that you can change, such as leaving a complicated relationship, or that you should acknowledge how they are, similar to a physical incapacity. If you can change the circumstance, your specialist will assist you with creating techniques for making the essential changes throughout your life as per your objectives and qualities. On the off chance that the issue is something that you can't transform, you can start to learn social techniques to work around your difficulties, so they don't have as quite a bit of a negative impact on your life.

When you have understood the present significant issues throughout your life, you and your specialist can start to assess any examples that have developed from quite a while ago. Along these lines, you can abstain from rehashing any negative patterns later on. Instead of battling with your feelings, you can figure out how to recognize them for what they are and figure out how to function with or around them to accomplish the satisfying life you need.

Benefit of ACT

The critical advantage of ACT is that it can assist patients with doing combating mental clutters like tension and melancholy without utilizing medicine. It trains patients to change how they identify with their negative musings and feelings, so these considerations don't dominate. While patients will be unable to dispose of every single pharmaceutical drug immediately, they might have the option to decrease their dose after some time, at last going off the prescription. With the narcotic emergency being such an intriguing issue in the clinical and psychological fields, it is promising to have compelling treatment choices that don't require drugs.

At its most essential level, ACT urges patients to acknowledge those things that are out of their control and focus on different contemplations and actions intended to improve their lives. Instead of feeling remorseful about having negative considerations or sentiments, patients discover that negative feelings are superbly common. At the point when they can acknowledge the negative pieces of their awareness, patients are all the more allowed to begin moving endlessly from them and towards a progressively positive course. The objective of ACT is to increment psychological flexibility. Practitioners assist patients with getting increasingly mindful of the manners in which they think and feel through care activities and techniques. They additionally center around making enduring conduct changes by focusing on new actions and considered designs. Patients figure out how to acknowledge their contemplations as they are and to assess those musings to decide if they are serving the patient's life objectives. On the off chance that the contemplations are not helping them, patients can work to ingrain new, progressively positive considerations and actions.

Acceptance and Commitment Therapy (ACT) is a special type of therapy that urges patients to grasp their negative musings and sentiments as opposed to attempting to keep away from or dispense with them. Prepared specialists utilize this strategy to treat a broad scope of conditions, and it has demonstrated to be surprisingly powerful for some individuals.

Mindfulness and ACT

Mindfulness is portrayed as keeping in touch with the present minute as opposed to floating off into a programmed pilot. Mindfulness permits a person to interface with the watching self, the part they know about, however, separate from the reasoning self. Mindfulness methods frequently assist individuals with expanding attention to every one of the five faculties just as of their contemplations and feelings.

Mindfulness likewise builds a person's capacity to withdraw from contemplations. Moves identified with painful emotions, desires, or circumstances are frequently first decreased and afterward, in the long run, acknowledged. Acceptance is the capacity to permit interior and outer experience to happen as opposed to battling or maintaining a strategic distance from the experience. On the off chance that somebody believes, "I'm a horrible individual," that individual may be asked instead to say, "I have the idea that I'm an awful individual." This adequately isolates the individual from the perception, subsequently stripping it of its negative charge.

At the point when individuals experience excruciating feelings, for example, tension, they may be told to open up, breathe into, or make space for the physical sentiment of uneasiness and permit it to stay there; similarly, all things considered, without fueling or limiting it.

CHAPTER - 8
STEPPING INTO FREEDOM-IDENTIFY

Much of the discussion of equality deals with that between individuals and is predicated on the assumption of a culturally equal society. It is, therefore, of limited help in engaging with intercultural equality or with equality between people belonging to diverse cultures. Equality requires the same treatment of people who are equal in relevant respects.

To treat them with the same regard, we have to be able to compare one with the other, yet to do so, according to the multiculturalists, is to force our viewpoint. The principle of difference cannot render any standards that oblige us to respect the "difference" of others. On what basis can they demand our regard, or we require theirs? It is very tough to support respect for difference without captivating to some postulates of equality or social fairness.

The idea of equality emerges from the fact that humans are political living things. As such, we possess the capacity to make different cultures; but this does not mean that all religions are equal. To change the idea of the equality of human beings with the concept of the balance of cultures does not accept the possibility of any social justice at all.

We must not accommodate the State's notion of diversity, capitalism's bastardization of justice, or the rehashing of the idea of "Britishness."

Human beings do share many capacities and needs in stock, but different cultures define these differences and develop new ones of their own. Since people are at once both similar and different, they should be attended to equally because of both. Such a belief, which grounds equality, not in human consistency but the interchange of uniformity and diversity, builds difference into the very idea of justice, breaks the traditional equation of equilibrium with similarity, and is immune to monist warp. Once the basis of equality turns, so does its content. Balance requires equal freedom or chances to be different, and attending to human beings equally requires us to take into point both their similarities and differences.

Sensitivity to differences is related to each of these levels. A simple example explains the point. It was recently seen that Asian candidates for jobs in Britain were systematically demerited because their habit of giving respect for their interviewers by not directly looking them in the eye led the latter to think that they were shifty and devious and are more likely to prove not so reliable. By failing to acknowledge the candidate's" system of meaning and cultural practices, interviewers ended up treating them unequally with their white equivalence. Understandably but wrongly, they thought that all human beings have and even perhaps ought to share an identical system of meaning which foreseeably turned out to be their own.

In a culturally homogenous world, individuals share broadly similar requirements, norms, motivations, social customs, and patterns of behavior. Equal rights mean more or less the same reasons, and equal treatment involves more or less equal treatment.

The doctrine of equality is therefore relatively easy to define and apply, and discriminatory divergence from it can be identified without much dissent. This is not the case only in a culturally differentiated society. Equality consists of equal treatment to those judged to be similar in relevant respects. Once we reckon cultural differences, equal treatment would mean not the same but differential treatment, raising the question as to how we can ensure that it is comparable across cultures and does not serve as a cloak for discrimination or privilege.

In multicultural societies, the way people dress often becomes a topic of the most heated and tenacious effort. As a condensed and visible sign of cultural identity, it matters much to the people involved, but also for that very reason, it awakens all manner of conscious and unconscious fears and bitterness within the broader society. It would not be too hard to suggest that acceptance of the diversity of dress in a multicultural society is a good indicator of whether or not the latter is at ease with itself. Equality and diversity are also essential components of health and social care. Excellent balance and diversity acts make sure that the services provided to people are fair and readily available to everyone.

Equality and diversity shouldn't be seen as bonus benefits to your health or social care setting but more as integral constituents.

Society is made up of a broad spectrum of human beings. Many differences are present in it, and these differences can create connections with one another, and they can also put certain groups at a demerit. This is called discrimination.

Discrimination can relate that individuals and whole groups are turned down from opportunities and treated differently and not reasonably based on specific features. Equality seeks to make sure that this does not happen at all. All groups and individuals should be treated "equally." Equality is about accepting diversity rather than forcing homogeneity.

The importance of favoring the rights of children and young people is that not all children are the same. They learn at different paces, and many need supports to help them, e.g., one to one teaching, speech therapy, disability problems, etc. They all deserve the right to learn and go to school they choose. Also, if you penalize a child because they come from a different background, this makes them feel unwanted.

Here are some steps you can take to promote cultural equity:

- Build cultural consciousness through substantive learning.
- Create and support programs to improve cultural leadership.
- Advocate for public and private-sectors that help cultural capital.
- Treating all workers and students equally.
- Creating an incorporating culture for all staff and students.
- Ensuring equal access to chances to enable students to take part in the learning process fully.

- Enabling everyone to expand to their maximum potential.

- Equipping staff and students with the power to challenge inequality and discrimination in their environment.

- Ensuring policies, procedures and processes don't discriminate.

- Treating everyone equally—For example, women must be treated the same and receive an equal salary as men.

- Forming a culture that is inclusive and welcoming to everyone—if an environment is not accepting an individual, the place must be adjusted. If this is not possible due to any reason, other options must be explored to find a solution to it. For example, providing wheelchair ramps for disabled people, prayer rooms, and breastfeeding spaces for lactating mothers, etc.

- Ensuring there is equal access to opportunities such as training, promotion, and learning available to everyone and that they can fully participate in these opportunities—this should be available to everyone and provided relatively and equally based on their skills and abilities.

CHAPTER - 9

HOW TO SUPPORT YOUR OWN HEALING?

Racial Trauma and Race Tool

Racial harassment is a type of racial trauma where someone's harassment focuses on race, ethnicity, or culture. Racial trauma and racial intimidation are wrong and you can get help to stop it.

Racial trauma and racist bullying may include:

- Personal attacks, including violence or attack
- Exclusion, different treatment or exclusion
- People who make assumptions about you because of your color, race or culture
- Racist jokes, including jokes about your race, race, or culture.

Racial trauma can affect everyone. It can make you feel that you are not important or do not fit in. You may feel sad, depressed, or angry. Even when not directed at you, it can be affected as if you heard someone discriminating against their culture. 4 things to remember:

You are not alone and there are ways to get support.

What Can You Do

If someone calls you by name, scares you, or acts unfairly, you can get help to stop this

Go away: If someone is racist towards you right now, stay away and don't retaliate or respond to stay safe.

Stay safe: Walk from school or university with someone you know and keep your phone charged. Calls to the emergency numbers are free.

Keep saying it: You may need to talk more than once about racial trauma or racist harassment. It is appropriate to tell someone else

Find someone to help you: It may take time to stop bullying. If you think a teacher does not want to help, you can talk to the manager.

How to Help a Friend

If you see or hear racial trauma, racist harassment, or discrimination, there are ways you can help.

Offer your support and tell your friend that what happened to them was wrong.

Ask your friend if he wants to report the incident. You can also offer to testify if you feel safe and comfortable.

Call the emergency services if you need the police or ambulance to keep your friend safe.

Take note of what you see and hear as soon as possible. This can be used as evidence or, if necessary, to make a police statement.

If it's safe to do so, talk. Keep calm and be assertive. You can say that you disagree with racist comments or jokes.

Why Are People Racist

Our thoughts and beliefs grow as they grow and are influenced by what we see and read in friends and family, neighborhoods, schools, and the media.

Racial trauma can sometimes start in response to world events or news. Other times, a certain racial individual who has had a painful personal experience with a rupee can blame anyone in that race.

Everyone makes assumptions. This can happen when they have no chance of winning over alternative opinions.

It is never appropriate to discriminate against someone by race. If you are concerned about how your views may affect other people, it may be helpful to imagine that you are someone else to try to see their views.

Speaking on Racial Trauma

There are things you can do to talk about racial trauma and racist harassment

- Don't accept racist jokes. Some persons can make racist jokes look good. Racist jokes are a kind of abuse and people can be injured even if they don't show that they are upset at the moment.
- Learn about other cultures and nationalities.
- If your friends are afraid to talk about it, ask about their culture or background for more information.
- Raising awareness of racial trauma and racist harassment.
- Participate in meetings and campaigns and educate others on the effects of racial trauma.

How to Teach Your Children About Racial Trauma

In a period of division, prejudice saturates our news streams and increases our anxiety.

Parents change their views on diversity and inclusion, concerned that their children are exposed from early childhood. But here is some hopeful news: You can resist the insidious extent of hatred before it's too late. We ask experts in child psychology and the fight against fanaticism to contextualize malicious events and beliefs, eliminate children's misunderstandings, and empower their children.

0-6 years – Study other cultures together by eating their food and watching their movies. Encourage your child's teacher to create multiculturalism in their curriculum. If you are bilingual, speak your native language or encourage your child to learn another language.

It is not necessary to tell a child of this age the bad of intolerance beforehand. It may be difficult to sit down with a 3-year-old and talk about racial trauma. But if the need arises to speak, tell me. "In 2017, we see a wave of bomb threats in Jewish community centers," says Jinnie Spiegler, curriculum and education manager for the League against Defamation. "On the news, very young children are being evacuated from these facilities. Of course, they knew something was wrong and I was afraid. Of course, you want to talk to them."

This may seem impossible, but the key is to keep the reach and language manageable to prevent racial trauma in children. Schonfeld usually says, the individual responsible must be very angry. Our words are used to solve problems. The speech may sound strange, but the worst part is silence.

6-8 years old – It's easier to talk openly about hate at this age, but I don't think it's a super formal talk. Many families or individuals unknowingly talk about these issues, says Allison Briscoe-Smith, a clinical psychologist in Berkeley, California, who specializes in addressing trauma to children and investigating how children understand race. "Young children adjust very fairly and unfairly. This is a solid basis for discussing injustice."

Children at this age can express their feelings, so the responsibility for directing speech should and should not rest entirely with you. It is advisable to inquire from him what he thinks about what he is hearing. What do people say in the playground? What did you see on television? Talk, security, honesty, and you can keep it at the right level of detail.

Don't overdo it. Just be simple, brief, and hones. If you feel reflective, the need to underestimate—"Those at the garlic festival can never be here"—avoid that. An empty word sounds like discontent, and if you are afraid of these events, you will feel that you are not taking them seriously. Instead, Dr. "Tell her exactly what you know: There are adults who love her and try to keep her safe," says Briscoe-Smith.

Children can have an interesting and real vision of the world and ask for something strange but important for their understanding.

9-11 years old – Child psychologists say that helping children cope with terrible events has become a very different task in recent years. The prevalence of technology allows children to be exposed to unprecedented information that is not mature enough to be meaningful. Turn off the TV; Do not allow children to access images of death." Briscoe-Smith. "But they have phones. You will see there and dozens of them on the screen. So we have to help them understand what they see and hear."

Even in security settings, sad news and unpleasant opinions will reach your child. Briscoe-Smith says: "My children tell me that the students at their school are joking with Latinos about ICE." If you run better, ICE will take you. Racial harassment has greatly increased in the past few years. I also ask, "What are people talking about at school, what does your phone say?"

This type of research is necessary, especially if you have an unnatural child. It may be difficult to rely on your kids to reveal disturbing things to you. "You have to ask. The rumors spread like wildfires at school and online. So help them fill in the blanks. You might say," I'm not sure this is the case in Minnesota, "before explaining how."

CHAPTER - 10
CONTRIBUTING FACTORS TO ETHNICITY AND RACIAL TRAUMA

A few components may add to the proposal that a few people are inalienably unrivaled or substandard. There are significantly two factors that offered ascend to racial trauma and ethnicity. They are: The Trans-Atlantic Slave Trade and Colonialism

The Trans-Atlantic Slave Trade

The supporters of slavery, including Christians, in this way, damaged the essential scriptural instructing that all humans are made in the picture of God and are in this manner equivalent (Gen. 1:26-28; acts 10:34). The assignment of Africans to a lower status of mankind was an outright dismissal for the picture of God in them. Numerous additionally contended for slavery on the premise that it was a practice in the Bible. Despite the fact that slavery was drilled in scriptural occasions (e.g., Exod. 21 and Lev. 25), there are striking differences among this and the slavery practices of the European and American slave owners.

How Can the Church Respond to Racial Trauma?

Ethnic, innate, and racial differences are a piece of the personality of every person. At the point when we become Christians, our social personalities are not destroyed, at the same time, as McGarry brings up, we are called to live above them: the supporters of Jesus are brought in the intensity of the Essence of God to beat any divisions that these attributes may have brought inside their own specific societies before they became Christians.

In conclusion, tribalism and racial trauma have adversely affected a lot of individuals in the Christian church, leaving their faith and expert morals compromised. This phenomenon isn't just corrupting, it is likewise disintegrating the authenticity and mission of the church. Tribalism, racial trauma, and different types of segregation are disruptive components to the body of Christ. Because of the childish inclinations of human instinct, tribalism and racial trauma are inconsistent with the Christian faith. The church won't become a model of unity and an indication of trust on the planet if tribalism and racial trauma inside its structures aren't valiantly tended to and disposed of as wrongdoing. What is unmistakably Christian untruths less in doctrinal and philosophical immaculateness, despite the fact that this is significant; what is particularly Christian is confirm in one's very own involvement in Jesus Christ, his changing affection, and the capacity to impart that adoration to other people, even with one's adversaries (Matt. 5:43-48).

What Is the Solution to Racial Trauma? Can People Be Taught to Not Be Racist?

The only true way to make a real and lasting change in how people think is by making some cultural changes. Societal norms and values need to undergo a real change. Today, people complain a lot about the culture promoting political correctness, but that simply creates a way to check people's attitudes and thoughts; both from outsiders and also a self-check.

Knowles concedes that changing norms can be an effective means to check violence stemming from racial trauma. However, to make a real change and unlearn the bias that most of us have been taught all of our lives, and make contact.

Can we expect that racial trauma will slowly disappear out of society with time? Can we agree that older people tend to be more racist, while the younger generation has a more open mind to diversity?

Richeson says that the idea that our country will gain some progress is simply a myth, and so is the idea that the younger generation will be our saviors. A majority of the hate group who sparked the Charlottesville violence were young white men.

She says that although data does show that younger groups like the millennials are more egalitarian and progressive in their thinking.

CHAPTER - 11
HOW TO STOMP OUT RACIAL TRAUMA

Forbid Racial Discourse and Supremacist Propaganda

Start by accepting that an absolutist free discourse convention that permits racist speech and propaganda isn't this brilliant and consecrated custom profiting everything except a wellspring of exemption. It enables racial trauma in a manner that is more extraordinary and destructive than anyplace else on the planet.

This isn't a misrepresentation. Just to give one model: there are two places on the planet where one can straightforwardly, openly take part in against Semitic discourse or Nazi purposeful publicity unafraid of government authorize. Those spots are the USA and Mid-Eastern nations.

The racial contempt that such a large number of individuals in the USA share isn't something new. It has been around since before the Common War when John C. Calhoun was a U.S. legislator and representative for the slave-ranch arrangement of the South made his scandalous "Slavery a Positive Good" discourse in 1837 in the US Senate.

Accurately in light of the fact that bigot discourse is secured political discourse, its memes could be passed on (since 1837) as a treasure from age to age.

The American free discourse convention depends on various profoundly imperfect premises including the Marketplace of Ideas doctrine. To cite Wikipedia:

The Marketplace of Ideas doctrine holds that reality will rise up out of the opposition of thoughts in free, straightforward open talk and reasons that thoughts and philosophies will be separated by their prevalence or mediocrity and far-reaching acknowledgment among the populace.

That didn't occur with racist thoughts. Following the Common War, free discourse made white supremacist propaganda that originally brought about bigot savagery and vigilantism, which caused the obliteration of Reconstruction, trailed by the foundation of

Isolation in the South. Persecution of African-Americans was in this manner continued by 100 years of supremacist propaganda, which was totally made conceivable by the absolutist free discourse custom.

In the 50 years, racial trauma in the US appeared in retreat. In all actuality, the reduction of racial trauma in the US occurred despite free discourse NOT as a result of it. It was NEVER the aftereffect of reality rising up out of the opposition of thoughts. Supremacist thoughts in the US were never "separated" in the 'commercial center of thoughts.'

The reduction of racial trauma was the consequence of legal activity by the US Supreme Court rendering Isolation and the concealment of the dark vote unlawful. This briefly crushed, confused, and dispirited profoundly imbued supremacist slant.

It was more the regard for the organization of law that brought liberation, than the marketplace of ideas encouraging kindly love. No big surprise that all it took for bigotry to return thundering to life was for one dark president to be voted into office followed by one terrible legislator who saw exposure esteem in straightforwardly rambling supremacist memes against Mexicans.

The bigot cops that are even today in our occasions shooting blacks in the back likely could be supremacist since they could openly soak up from the wellspring of bigot discourse. Had there been less supremacist discourse, perhaps, quite possibly, some of them may never have gotten either racist or been fewer supremacists. That could conceivably have made a couple of fewer lives be lost to contempt.

Protecting abhor discourse is over the top. Judges today don't confide in the marketplace of ideas to administer bad-to-the-bone sex entertainment. How is supremacist discourse or publicity prevalent that it ought to appreciate more insurance than in-your-face sex entertainment? Why this glaring irregularity? Truth be told, consuming a wooden cross on an African-American family's yard is as yet ensured political discourse, in the event that we tail US Incomparable Court law. To cite Wikipedia:

R.A.V. v. City of St. Paul, 505 U.S. 377 (1992), is an instance of the US Incomparable Court wherein the Supreme Court collectively struck down St. Paul's Predisposition Spurred Wrongdoing Law and turned around the conviction of a young person, alluded to in court archives just as R.A.V., for consuming a cross on the garden of an African-American family for damaging the Primary Correction's assurances for the right to speak freely of discourse.

A lot of whites don't have faith in the expression "white benefit." On the off chance that you are a less taught white male who loses his employment in reality as we know it where there are a decreasing number of very much compensated occupations for less instructed individuals, and you can't locate another well-paying employment that will shield your wife from leaving you, you can't be sensibly called special. However, it is likewise evident that this white male, anyway hopeless, is probably not going to EVER be the object of racist propaganda.

In the event that you are white, knowledgeable, and sensibly prosperous, let say an established legal advisor or an appointed authority, it will be a songbird to praise the marketplace of ideas teaching: you will NEVER be the object of supremacist discourse.

In the event that you are dark, knowledgeable, and sensibly prosperous, let say an established legal advisor or an appointed authority, you can, in any case, get shot in the back by a racist cop who may have taken an interest in a racial oppressor tiki burn walk yelling supremacist trademarks.

In the event that you were a knowledgeable, prosperous white individual and some outsider would approach you and strike you over the mouth and just leave leaving you remaining there, you would presumably be damaged forever. And afterward, you have the nerve to commend an alleged "rule" that honestly does that mentally to non-white individuals.

Shielding a free discourse custom that secures racist discourse isn't protecting equality, dignity, or justice. It is straightforward as it can be guarding racial oppression. Also, racial oppressors know it. They esteem and value this free discourse convention. They simply love it. Good sense should direct supporters of the absolutist free discourse convention to recollect Kant's adage:

With Companions Like These, Who Needs Adversaries?

Obviously, we realize this isn't what was proposed. Also, we know most supporters of the absolutist free discourse convention have good intentions. However, there is a thing called the unintended result. Thus one more precept:

The way to damnation is cleared with honest goals.

Stop Discrimination

Quit dividing individuals by race. Do away with multi-culturalism. Not any more African Americans, not any more Asian Americans, not any more Hispanic Americans. We are

Americans... period. We don't learn in school in various dialects. We teach in schools in the national language... English! People groups head will detonate over that one yet to bring together the nation; we need a national language to help bind together us.

We stop isolating into little Italy, Chinatown, little Mexico, and so forth. Live any place you need...!

Racial trauma separates us by race just as we are unique. Invert segregation is still Separation! Treat everybody similarly... similar rights, similar obligations.

Dispose of black history month. Show black history with white history, Asian and Hispanic history. It's classified as "History."

To put it plainly, the manner in which you battle racial trauma is by not making everything about race. Also, for the individuals who like to mark others as racists... that is almost outlandish for them!

Since meritocracy is as a rule progressively rubbished, it's about time the idea that diversity is a higher priority than merit went standard.

At the point when individuals from favored classes need to reply to individuals from the persecuted classes for their activities, responsibility will consequently increase no matter how you look at it, radically decreasing prejudice.

For instance, an Indian living in the US you never need to stress over a cop misjudging your goals when you are pulled over. You might never know about police mercilessness against Indians; in any event insufficient to lose your cool when you see a cop. On the off chance that anything, you've known about stories where police demonstrated additional tolerance towards Indians.

The explanation is that Indians are spoken to be among the exclusive classes of US society. The CEOs of the best 2 tech organizations Google and Microsoft are Indian. We have Indian legislators like Bobby Jindal. Indians are generalized as a rich over-class of Designers and Specialists. They are scarcely spoken to among crooks. In this way, cops will in general expect that Indians are innocuous, coming about in far fewer shooting occurrences on their part. The same goes for Japanese and Koreans rather than Nigerians or Liberians.

Portrayal in great spots will naturally assume a job in stifling troublesome yet certain predispositions; among having numerous different advantages.

Would you like to fix racial trauma? Then prioritize diversity.

De-Programming Our Minds

I would harp Americans each opportunity I got that the explanation there is a supremacist framework here is on the grounds that we were balkanized–isolated and won. We were hoodwinked by the balkanizers to see each other as alternate extremes; consequently, the best approach to vanquish the racial trauma is to de-program ourselves from seeing each other as contrary energies. What's more, I mean everyone. The supposed "white" individuals have been addressed for my entire life to quit generalizing the alleged individuals of color. The following stage is to begin pestering the supposed "individuals of color" to do likewise. There are immense profits directly around the bend!

It was the 1670's. The constrained workers from Europe had quite recently collaborated with the constrained workers from Africa and practically toppled the legislature. The administration at that point did the main assignment part of its expected set of responsibilities; it partitioned the two by advancing those from Europe into the slave master class, the exemplary vocation way in these circumstances. American racial trauma was conceived.

People have extreme impulses that help this sort of structure. These are the impulses that empower a populace that considers it to be more grounded than another, to feel scorn towards those "others," at that point to attack and belittle them and move all fault onto them. When the powerless sub-gathering (or neighbors) has been handled along these lines, it's extremely simple for the perpetrator gathering to either take up arms and dispense with them, or make a psychological oppressor state undermining demolition, and subjugate them.

These impulses go path back to when various leveled societies initially developed and realms started to shape. There are excesses of plot focuses and bits of discourse that you find springing up anyplace on the planet this procedure unfurls, practically verbatim. IMO, human intuition is much increasingly noticeable, way more mind-boggling than we comprehend by any means.

Recall how racists were doing personifications of Barack and Michelle, making them look like gorillas? In 1992, a writer from Los Angeles was in Croatia. He knew two Serbian ladies who were working in a primary school. The main explanation they had those occupations was that nobody realized they were Serbs. The two detailed how much tormenting was going on, that different instructors were encouraging. The youngsters provoked any kid they knew to be Serb with how monstrous Serbs are and that they look like gorillas.

CHAPTER - 12
CAUSES AND EFFECTS OF RACIAL TRAUMA

If we're going to effectively tackle the problem of racial trauma and eventually uproot it from our way of living and thinking, then it is definitely important to dive into the causes of racial trauma. When we can identify the cause, we can find ways to make the real changes that are desperately needed.

The Main Causes of Racial Trauma

1. An Instinctive Feeling of Responsibility to Protect One's Social Race

It is instinctive to feel connected to anyone with whom we feel similar. It's normal to feel a certain level 0f comfort when we are among people who reflect us in behavior and appearance. Humans are easily triggered by anything that threatens to put anything we care about, from our territory to family to identity and culture, in harm's way. Racial trauma is the extreme and misdirected form of human nature to protect anything we deem valuable. So, if something or someone doesn't seem to fit into the same group, they are quickly perceived as a threat, inferior, or both.

2. Fear of Displacement and Loss

Humans are instinctive protectors of their own people and position, which means that they fear any loss of either or both of those things. It ranges from social status to possessions, territory, and even jobs. Humans are naturally afraid of being displaced by anyone who seems better and more appealing than they are. When you are replaced by someone better than you, you feel unworthy, don't you? This is not an attempt to justify racial trauma, but fear is one of its biggest and worst sponsors. Nobody wants to lose anything. Not people, not a territory, and definitely not their rights.

3. Ignorance

This is the product of being unaware, uninformed, or uneducated, and this drives racial trauma even in the 21st century. Being raised a certain way all your life, and watching everyone around you function the same way can fool you into believing a thing to be right despite it being morally wrong. Having another human being who doesn't share the same sentiments as you can make you feel a little uneasy sometimes. So many people don't see their actions, thoughts, and words as racist, because they genuinely believe they are correct. Putting an end to this ignorance can only be done by creating awareness, educating people on the errors of their ways, as well as the consequences that follow. Until ignorance is uprooted by proper education, racial trauma will continue to eat deep into the hearts of humans.

4. A Lack of Self-Love and the Desire to Feel Worthy and Superior

The most racist of the bunch tend to be the ones without self-confidence, any kind of esteem, and—chief of all—self-love. A racist persona projects all that negative energy onto people that are considered vulnerable, inferior, and weak. You can only truly appreciate another person if you truly love and appreciate everything that you are. Racial trauma is rooted in feelings of worthlessness, envy, and feelings of victimization. Some people tend to take out their failures on other people, and racists are no different. Racists are usually filled with feelings of insignificance, isolation, being unloved, and offended, leading them to put all that energy into blaming and hating another person. Racial trauma is an individual act that can only be fixed by confronting these individual feelings and actions.

5. Having a Pro-Racist Family Background

Parents have more impact on their children's thoughts and beliefs than they might realize. Children note down their parent's reactions to a person from another race and work to emulate it without even feeling the need to know why. If a white parent treats an Asian American harshly in front of their child, the child simply assumes that it was the right course of action. After all, "Mommy did it." Hate is born in the family and can be hard to correct. Upbringing plays an important role in your personality and values.

6. Pressure from Friends

People are easily influenced by peer pressure more than they realize, and even as significantly as they are influenced by their parents. You are more likely to listen to the people you have chosen as your friends, which means you are also more inclined to agree with things they say—and that includes views on people of color. This is a major cause of racial trauma.

7. Personal Experiences

If you have ever experienced any form of assault from a member of a certain race, there's a high chance that you end up living in fear of the entire race. It is completely normal for people to feel this way. It is what happens after you get heartbroken or betrayed by someone you cared about. There's a good chance you develop a strong opinion against that person's culture, and not a good one. This fear, this survival instinct, can manifest as racial trauma and impair your judgment.

8. Stereotypes

This is a major cause of racial trauma. It is conveyed through radio, music, television, books, and, most importantly, the internet. Stereotyping believes all members of a group think and act the same way because of how a member behaves or is portrayed. Whenever an impressionable person is introduced to stereotypes or people who have been stereotyped, they quickly conclude that other people in that category must act and think alike. People of color have been stereotyped all over the world, and the younger generation is picking up on these cues.

9. Unfamiliarity

This is another common cause of racial bias. There are people who live in fear of the unknown. Anything they don't know or understand is a source of fear for them, and that includes people of other cultures. A child who is raised and surrounded by only people from their race has the possibility of becoming racist. That possibility increases when they have been fed with negative stereotypes about other races.

This isn't necessarily what happens every time, but when combined with stereotyping and a lack of experience with other races, it slowly builds into a racist mentality. For this reason, children must be taught and be allowed to experience diversity so that their minds can absorb the right information and build a solid anti-racist foundation in preparation for the future.

The Effects of Racial Trauma

First, let's address the effects of racial trauma on society. A society powered by a racist mentality restricts some citizens from participating and contributing to the collective progress of the nation, and this puts a damper on development and success. If a good amount of a society's population does not have access to the same privileges as the others, they will always be a few steps behind. Victims of racial trauma tend to lack employment and academic opportunities that would have given them the chance to give back to society, ensuring the overall wellbeing of the country's economy.

Another thing to note is that discriminating against an entire race limits them from fully being a part of the country's culture. This causes other citizens to not fully appreciate the differences and similarities among them, which results in social inactivity and the continuation of racial trauma in the future.

Living comfortably with racial trauma keeps the country at a disadvantage because the result will be aggression, cruelty, and sheer violence on a national or local scale. If bad blood is allowed to accumulate between groups in the community, it's a one-way street to isolated incidents, verbal and physical confrontations, and other forms of low-level negativity. Racial intolerance and discrimination are a recipe for riots, fights, and even war.

Racial trauma also has effects on an individual level. Individuals who are faced with racial bias every day find that their lives become very restricted. Fear becomes an all too familiar feeling, with low self-esteem as a regular side effect. When a person experiences persecution and discrimination every day of their life, they eventually come to the conclusion that they are as unworthy as people say, and this only works in favor of the oppressors.

Anyone who attributes little value to themselves almost never makes an effort to achieve more than they already have, and this leads to family generation drenched in disadvantages. Also, it is common for victims of racial trauma to grow into resentful, defensive, and aggressive individuals who look to criminal activity as a way to rebel against injustice. However, this just serves to keep them at a disadvantage.

Another tragic effect of racial trauma is death through hate crimes and police brutality, which often appears to have no consequences. Countless people have died because society saw their lives as inferior and insignificant, and these deaths affect more than just the person who died. That person was a parent, a spouse, an uncle or aunt, a friend, a colleague, and so on. Imagine being murdered just for having the "wrong" skin color.

CHAPTER - 13

IDENTIFYING THE PROBLEM

The easiest way to learn how to be confident and overcome low self-esteem is to pinpoint their root causes and put an end to them. You cannot find solutions without identifying first what the problems are. Otherwise, the psychological cycle of your ebbing confidence will continue to haunt you until you are back to square one.

The problem is in your mind, so might as well go directly to the problem—an easy and simple but effective rule.

Ironic, but the easiest way of overcoming low self-esteem is also the hardest part for many people. Their judgments are clouded by self-deprecating thoughts, so they fail to weigh things objectively from a standpoint that does not count emotions and baseless interpretations. They tend to believe what they want to believe and not what other people are really saying about them. That is because their minds amplify the wrongs and dismiss the rights as futile and trifle.

People who clearly see their flaws are usually those who fail to notice their real beauties. Being keen about their own qualities could have been a great requisite for self-awareness, but the real problems with most people who lack confidence and possess low self-esteem are in their heads. Their minds are their own big enemies. They create their own problems that in effect harm their self-esteem.

More than a real physical state, the usual root causes of low self-esteem are mere characteristics taking the form of mindsets resulting from either actual experiences of embarrassment and humiliation or wrong concepts of self-importance and beauty. These purely fictional mental stories, sometimes just isolated cases, are adapted as truth—pseudo-truths that end with disastrous situations, more often than not.

There are a lot of self-help solutions that you can apply and live up to, but without knowing your real self-first, your weaknesses will remain where they are, waiting to deliver your next defeat. After identifying the real problems—negative mindsets and emotions—the next step is realization. You have to realize that they are nothing but products of your playful imagination, and a result of not believing enough in yourself.

Do a personal assessment to know where your problems are coming from. Here are the most common culprits in lower self-esteem.

1. Perfectionism

- Do you set incredibly high standards in everything you do even if it means setting aside realistic measures?

- Do you believe that things will always go according to your plans and expectations like you completely control them?

- Do you think that committing mistakes define who you are and that mistakes decide for your real value?

- Do you believe that only perfection is acceptable in everything?

If you answer yes to most of the questions, then that means you are very prone to experiencing low self-esteem due to unexpected failures. What flies high, falls harder. A perfect life complete with perfect decisions and a perfect world around you is nothing but an ideal dream that will never turn into reality.

You are bound to commit mistakes one time or another simply because you are human who does not control everything. When that time comes and your perfectionism finds its way to mess up your head, you will feel more down, disappointed, and depressed than normal. It will make you feel that you lose everything, including your pride and self-worth. Your self-esteem will suffer for nothing.

To correct this way of thinking, start believing that committing mistakes is not the end for you— that you are not defined by your mistakes but by your correct decisions and how you stand up after every fall. If things do not seem attainable, simply adjust your standards to become more realistic. If you cannot be perfect, just be the best. Real confidence is shown by how you compose yourself after failing once, ready to bounce back.

2. Neurotic guilt

- Do you not forgive yourself for not being perfect and committing mistakes?

- Do you dwell on the results of your bad decisions that you already fail to find solutions to make up for them?

- Do you tend to exaggerate the consequences of your bad decisions from what they actually are?

If so, you most probably have low self-esteem because you cannot let go of your transient flaws. You have no confidence to go out and take a risk because you are afraid that the guilt will haunt you once again.

This state of mind is called neurotic because it is recognized as a disorder that can result in Generalized Anxiety Disorder (GAD) or Post-Traumatic Stress Disorder (RACIAL TRAUMA).

Do not be guilty of not being the best or most beautiful. Be guilty of not loving yourself and believing that you are special in your own way. Do not be ashamed of yourself because you will never be the unluckiest person in the world. If you have weaknesses, you surely have strengths as well.

Guilt will never fix your wrong decisions in the past, so what good does it give? Guilt does not act by itself; it is you who needs to work to make yourself better in the inside and outside.

3. Hypersensitivity to criticism

- Do you feel bad even for little criticisms and constructive criticisms?

- Do you think that all opinions directed to you are out of malice?

Hypersensitivity lowers self-esteem because you are easily influenced by other people's opinions about you rather than believing in yourself first to validate if what they think has a basis. It also implies low self-respect and self-worth. What makes this characteristic emotionally harmful, is that it sways a person towards negativity, breaking whatever little self-esteem is existing.

To overcome this, always objectively assess yourself first and see if what they say is right. Do not involve emotions just yet. If you think they are wrong, prove them wrong. Show them that you are not what they say you are by composing yourself and performing better. You have more to prove, so you also have more reasons to believe in yourself.

4. Self-criticism

- Do you criticize yourself for achieving less?
- Do you dislike yourself for not being what you want to be?
- Do you think other people are better than you?
- Do you punish yourself for every mistake and failure?

Heavy self-criticism also depletes your confidence because you only see your flaws, which eventually, gives you the impression that you will never be good enough. Most often than not, self-criticism is a kind of destructive criticism. It brings you down but does not allow you to get up and give yourself a second chance.

Self-criticism is the opposite of self-awareness. The latter makes you comfortable in your own skin, flawed or not, while the former just highlights your weaknesses with no intent to improve. Self-criticism is a mere act of reprimanding yourself to a point of emotional damage. It does not change anything—acting does.

Act to improve what you think you lack in. Do not self-criticize but only remind yourself that you need to change for the better. Criticism is futile if you won't act on it.

5. Invidiousness

- Do you always feel discontented with your own looks and achievements?

Discontentment breeds a lot of negative emotions that build up inside you—enviousness, malice, and resentment. You fail to see the line between good and bad. When that happens, self-esteem suffers a heavy blow because the concept of self-worth is also blurred.

Take away that animosity you throw yourself for being discontented. Discontentment is just mere mental and emotional limitations, not a real one determined by your own skills and abilities. Take inspiration from successful people who did not make it big-time for the first time but still ended up being successful.

6. Envy

- Do you wish you are somebody else or someone like you know?
- Do you always think that other people are better than you?
- Do you keep a grudge for people you deeply envy?

This way of thinking implies resentment of oneself that the person already wishes to be somebody else, somebody that is better in his eyes. He often wants the possessions and qualities that other people have because he thinks that he cannot be a better person without them. Hence, he fails to see his own qualities that also make him special in the eyes of others.

It is okay to admire other people and want to have the things and qualities that make them stand out. It is a goal that will make you a better person. But if achieving that goal means forsaking yourself, then, you are definitely going the wrong way.

But then again, if you will not let go of your hypersensitivity, you will just see every opinion about you in a negative light.

7. Pessimism

- Do you tend to think negatively when trying to grasp a situation?

- Do you believe negative possibilities more than you do with positive possibilities?

- Do your sense of hope already wanes in your first unsuccessful attempt?

Pessimism instills fear which in effect weakens resolve and renders natural skills and abilities less efficient because of the conscious belief that everything is bound to fail anyway. It manifests through personality, manner of speaking, attitude, and physical appearance. The negativity inside your head holds you back, robbing your confidence and hindering you from giving your best all the time because you believe that regardless of efforts, the outcome will still be the same.

This is a time when low self-esteem becomes palpable, transcending from being a mere emotion and state of mind to actions that everybody can see and feel, proving that perhaps, you are really what naysayers are saying about you.

Negativity spreads like a virus. Do not influence other people with your pessimism. Believe that the possibility of failure is the same as the possibility of success. Throw in more resolve and well-thought actions, and you are bound to succeed even more. There is no point in guessing outcomes anyway, so might as well be confident that things will be in your favor.

8. Floating Hostility

- Do you harbor ill will every time somebody gives you advice and critique?
- Do you hate or get mad at every person who gives you criticisms, constructive or destructive?

If you think they clearly describe who you are, then, floating hostility could be an underlying cause of your lack of confidence and low self-esteem. This is a defensive mechanism that people subconsciously activate to show that their critiques are wrong. However, instead of proving them wrong, they welcome the criticisms with hostility in the false hopes that it will make them look stronger and tougher.

Unfortunately, this defensive mechanism is seen by other people as a sign of your inability to admit the truth, which is vital in changing what is there to be changed for the better. As a result, you fail to act on the criticisms, so your flaws remain, which through time will continue to damage your self-esteem and confidence.

Do not deny criticisms if you think they have a basis. Otherwise, you will just deny the opportunity to grow and improve.

9. Chronic Indecision

- Can't you decide on your own using your own discretion?

- Do you often rely on the decisions of others to make your own?

- Do you not trust your own choices?

CHAPTER - 14

WHAT IS ANTI-RACIAL TRAUMA?

In general, anti-racial trauma promotes an equal society in which people are not discriminated against on the basis of race. Movements such as the civil rights movement and the anti-apartheid movement are examples of anti-racist movements. Peaceful resistance is generally praised as an active element of anti-racist movements, although this has not always been the case. Hate crimes, positive discrimination and the prevention of racist discourse are also examples of government policies that attempt to combat racial trauma.

The Policy of Racial Segregation

It is an official policy based on the distinction between the treatment of blacks and whites on the one hand and Europeans on the other, in the areas of housing, education, employment, and transport and leisure facilities. It began in Africa, when European colonialism existed, with a policy of apartheid following the declarations of Cecil Rhodes and Daniel François Malan Club (1875-1954), and conceived the word "apart," meaning separation or segregation; in South Africa, the 1910 Constitution lost its constitution, which limited parliamentary representation to Europeans only and deprived Africans of the right to vote.

In 1950, a law was passed that assigns places to black and white people and forces them to erect barriers. In the regions where they live, Africans fought the policy of apartheid with strikes, protests, and conferences, and the Republic of South Africa was criticized by the Commonwealth countries and withdrew from the Commonwealth in 1961 instead of changing its policy, and the United Nations General Assembly condemned it in November 1962 and called for sanctions to be imposed. It asked the Security Council to consider excluding her from the UN, and European governments and peoples opposed her policy, and sanctions were imposed on the country of South Africa until the laws were changed and Africans were given their rights.

The policy of racial discrimination was also found in Rhodesia (now Zimbabwe), Kenya, Uganda, and America, particularly in the southern states, and this policy began in America after the American Civil War and the emergence of racist laws that abolished white control in the late

19th century. Martin Luther King urged blacks not to use violence to express their anger and resistance to apartheid, and in 1955 and 1956 he led the Black County movement for a bus in Montgomery, the capital of Alabama, after a black woman named Rosa Parks was invited, to give their place to a white man on the bus, and refused, and the boycott continued until the Supreme Court issued a decision repealing the isolation laws, Martin Luther King was killed, but the apartheid movement in America was active, especially after the passage of the CR Act in 1964.

Racial Trauma in the United States

White Americans were given privileges and rights that were reserved for them alone without any other races. European Americans (especially Anglo-Saxon white Protestants) were granted exclusive privileges in the United States.

Tasks in the areas of education, immigration, region, elections, citizenship, and possession of urine throughout this history. Non-Protestant immigrants who emigrated from Europe, especially Irish, Polish, and Italian, often suffered from the exclusion of foreigners and other forms of discrimination in American society until the end of your 19th and beginning of the 20th years. In addition, American groups in the Middle East, such as Jews and Arabs, faced persistent discrimination in the United States, so that these individuals, who belong to these groups, are not identified as persons with white skin color. Immigrants from South, East, and Southeast Asia have also faced racial discrimination in the United States.

Major institutions based on race and ethnicity include slavery and apartheid, detention of American Indians, residential schools, the Immigration and Naturalization Act, and detention camps. Racial discrimination was officially prohibited in the mid-twentieth century and was considered socially and morally unacceptable, but racial policy remains an important phenomenon and continues to be reflected in social and economic inequality. Racial class continues to exist in employment, housing, education, loans, and government.

The United Nations and the American Human Rights Network believe that "discrimination in the United States permeates all aspects of life and extends to all non-white races." The nature of the views of ordinary Americans has changed dramatically. Surveys conducted by organizations such as ABC News over the past few decades have revealed that large sectors of Americans recognize the adoption of discriminatory perspectives even in modern America, with the exception of the example mentioned in an article published by ABC

In 2007, one in 10 Americans admitted to being prejudiced against Latin Americans and Latinos, and one in four admitted to being prejudiced against Arab Americans. A 2018 YouGov/Economist poll found that 17 percent of Americans oppose marriage between two different races, 19 percent oppose marriage to "other" groups, 18 percent oppose marriage to blacks, 17 percent refuse to marry whites, and 15 percent refuse to marry Latinos.

Some Americans say that Barack Obama's candidacy for the presidency as the first black and United Nations president for two consecutive presidential terms from 2008 to 2016 was proof that the nation is entering a new era (the post-racist era). "Now we are in the 100era old, system-partisan, system -racial society," said right-wing populist presenter Le Doubs in November 2009. Two months after these comments, Chris Matthews, an MSNBC presenter, commenting on Obama's success in the presidential election, the television station said, "It's really a time after all, as you know, I forgot for an hour that I was black tonight. Some analysts have viewed the election of Donald Trump as president, as well as the election of the United States in 2016, as a racist response to the election of Barack Obama.

American society continued to suffer from high levels of racial trauma and discrimination during the first decade of the third millennium, and one of the new phenomena in society has been the emergence of the Right Alternative Movement, which is a white nationalist alliance that seeks to expel sexual and racial minorities from the United States.

In August 2017, these groups participated in a march in Charlottesville, Virginia, and the various white nationalist factions united against ethnic minorities. During the march, a white racist demonstrator drove his car into an anti-demand group, killing one person and injuring 19 others. Since mid-2010, the Department of Homeland Security and Federal Investigations has identified white racial violence as the main domestic terrorist threat in the United States.

CHAPTER - 15

SOLIDARITY AGAINST RACIAL TRAUMA

That the first black president of the United States will pass the command to a successor accused of racist attitudes by critics and supported by nationalist whites, seems an irony of fate.

But that is the bitter drink that awaits Barack Obama when his historic presidency ends on January 20, and Donald Trump takes his place.

The Obama presidency was a real milestone for the United States. From the day that, some years ago, he settled with his family in a White House built by slaves.

That fact in a country so marked by slavery and racial strife-filled many around the world with pride and hope, and not only blacks.

However, a question now arises as Obama's term expires: did he comply with the black community in the US?

Obama said in his speech that progress could be seen "not only in statistics" but "in the attitudes of the young Americans across the political spectrum."

Blacks, along with Hispanics in the U.S., were the group where poverty fell the most in 2015 from the other year, according to census data released in September.

That fall of more than two percentage points was important since blacks account for 24.1% of the poor in this country, and together with Hispanics, they account for 45.5% of the total.

Also, both groups were among those who saw the largest increase in their income.

Those figures reflected the economic growth and job growth achieved after the great recession that Obama inherited.

But they were also the result of government programs. In many societies and the world, but not everywhere, right-wing ideas, conservative and reactionary, are advancing. They want to impose a story of the world, relayed by an overwhelming action of all the means of communication like the story of the only possible world. This push from the right and the far right is the result of an offensive systematically carried out in several directions. We will retain six complementary offensives.

The second offensive is military, police, and judicial; it has taken the form of the destabilization of restive territories, the multiplication of wars, the instrumentalization of terrorism. It continued in police violence, the criminalization of social and citizen movements and solidarity movements. The third offensive focused on work, with the questioning of job security and widespread casualization, by the subordination of science and technology, especially digital and biotechnology, to the logic of financialization. The fourth offensive was waged against the welfare state through financialization, commodification, and privatization; it has resulted in the widespread corruption of the political classes. The fifth offensive, following the fall of the Berlin Wall in 1989, concerned the attempt to disqualify progressive, socialist, or communist projects. The sixth offensive is geopolitical. It seeks to reconsider decolonization and prevent its further development and development. It directly attacks international law by subordinating it to business law and the supremacy of the former colonial powers.

The offensive of the dominant oligarchy scored points, but it did not cancel the resistances. The points of view which advocate emancipation remain strong, and there are even new counter-tendencies. The movements that started in 2011 in Tunis remain lively and are renewed, as we can see with the movements in Algeria, Sudan, and elsewhere. The watchwords are clear; it is a rejection of social misery and inequality, respect for freedoms, dignity, rejection of forms of domination, the link between ecological emergency and social emergency. From one movement to another, there have been refinements on the accusation of corruption, on-demand for "real democracy," on ecological constraints, land grabbing, and control of raw materials.

In several of these movements, the classical left is defeated, and the right currents sometimes manage to capture the rejection of the dominant order. This is what happens when the left relays the conceptions of the right on precariousness, inequality, identity, security, discrimination, racial trauma. We must insist on the new issue, the rejection of corruption, the rejection of the political classes' merger, and the financial classes which cancel the autonomy of the political and cause mistrust of the people about the political authorities.

The rise of racist, security, xenophobic ideologies characterizes counter-revolutions. It takes concrete form in the offensives against migrants, based on racial trauma and xenophobia. Neoliberalism hardens its domination and strengthens its security character supported by repressions and coups. Social movements and citizens find themselves in a defensive position. But, in the medium term, nothing is played.

We must return to the current situation to take stock of the consequences of a period of conservative counterrevolutions: the neoliberal counterrevolution, that of the old and new dictatorships, that of evangelical conservatism, that of Islamist conservatism, that of conservatism Hindu. She recalls that revolutionary periods are generally short and often followed by violent and much longer counterrevolutions. But counter-revolutions do not cancel revolutions, and what is new continues to progress and emerges, sometimes long after, in new forms.

The authoritarian and violent evolution of neoliberalism is neither fortuitous nor temporary. By losing its alliance with the middle classes and certain popular strata which had operated at the time of the New Deal, neoliberalism, after the 2008 crisis, turns its back on a democratic option, even a relative one; he engages in an austerity version, mixing austerity with authoritarianism and developing aggressive state violence.

About the emergencies and the dangers of totalitarian escalations that occupy the philosophical and political space, the alliance between humanists and radical alternatives is essential. It requires renewal and a reinvention of humanism, in the sense of a philosophy which aims at the development of the human person and the respect of his dignity. It recalls the importance and the fruitfulness of the debates which have illustrated, among others, Christian humanism and theology of liberation, resistance to Stalinism in Marxist thought, criticism of Western universalism, proposals for an evolutionary and ecological humanism. It becomes necessary to invent how alter-globalism is humanism.

The victory of totalitarian tendencies was acquired at the level of ideas and ideologies. The far-right began its offensive against equality in the late 1970s. In France, in association with circles in the United States, the Clock Club has carried out, with the help of scientists and intellectuals, an offensive way to assert that equality is not natural and that these are inequalities. This offensive targeted freedom defending only corporate freedom and fought international law in its reference to the Universal Declaration of Human Rights. The choice of war against migrants is part of the far right of the war against equality, freedom, and fundamental rights.

This offensive attacked internationalism by highlighting neoliberal capitalist globalization supported by the rise of identity nationalism. Faced with this offensive, globalist and the recognition of multiple identities, proposed by Edouard Glissant, would make it possible to go beyond the confrontation between nationalism and globalism. Multipolarity would make it possible to overcome the still living contradictions between North and South. Altermondialism also highlights the complementarity between local, national, and global approaches. There is no impossible contradiction between these approaches. The local implies the link between the territories and the democratic institutions of proximity, the redefinition of the municipals of emancipation. The national level implies the redefinition of politics.

Racial trauma and xenophobia, well-fueled, are among the main weapons of domination. The current phase of capitalist globalization, neoliberalism, has exploded inequalities. Inequalities build on and reinforce discrimination. Racial trauma makes people accept discrimination; it also promotes precariousness, poverty, and exploitation. The stakes are twofold for the dominant. First of all, it is a question of limiting resistance to capitalism, of dividing the popular strata and rallying the middle strata; it is also a question of closing the alternatives by calling into question the value of equality.

We thus find Gramsci's explanations of the importance of cultural hegemony, which allows a system of domination to impose itself and be accepted by the dominated social strata. In this cultural battle, the definition of a project, carrying an emancipation alternative, is essential. It is an exercise in a democracy which contributes to its renewal—an essential step to discover and invent new paths.

We respond that anti-racial trauma is a fundamental positive value. For it to play its role, we must accept to look at what racial trauma and discrimination have marked in our societies, which continues to characterize them. They are found in various forms through the different versions of racial trauma, anti-Arab, anti-Maghreb, Islamophobia, anti-Semitic; sexism; colonization and de-alienation of the colonizers; the vivid memory of slavery and the slave trade; colonialist which marks the nature of the state; racialization of policies; the treatment of migrants and Roma as scapegoats ... These are not miasmas from the past, which are of little importance. Nor are they secondary contradictions that will disappear on their own after economic and social liberation. These are buttresses and buttress arches that hold the dominant system and reproduce it.

The emancipation project must be an alternative; emancipation integrates and strengthens the different liberations. The strategic orientation is that of access for all too fundamental rights, which requires the co-construction of a new universalism. Other liberations are preparing to occupy the scene of emancipation. Profound, fundamental upheavals are taking place in our societies. The women's rights revolution is progressing despite terrible resistance. The revolution of the rights of peoples confronted with the second phase of decolonization, that of the transition from the independence of States to the liberation of peoples. The ecological revolution which functions like a philosophical revolution requiring to redefine emancipation. The digital revolution and biotechnologies are changing language, writing, and the definition of the human—the demographic revolution and, in particular, the migrations which are upsetting the population of the planet.

CHAPTER - 16

HYPOCRISY WITHIN US

We all have inner conflicts and thoughts that clash with our actions and vice versa. We have all, at times, wanted to achieve a particular goal but have been counterproductive in our daily actions. It is not enough to just wish a particular thing into existence. We must do the work necessary to achieve what we claim we want. There are also those of us who pretend, who put on a façade and act like this is who we are. But we know we are really playing a game, and our true goals are the opposite of that which we are trying to convince others. You can't claim to be a vegetarian but love your mom's meatloaf. You can't claim to be a libertarian but push for all-out war against those who you don't agree with. You can't claim that you love everybody, but hate someone that did something against you. There is hypocrisy within us all and we must address ourselves as the first obstacle to achieve a better way of life.

Look in the Mirror

I am not ashamed to say that the reason people are being oppressed in this country is that there is a people ruling over us, oppressing us with a system of racial trauma that is obvious. But we need to talk about the reason we have allowed ourselves to remain in this condition for four hundred years. We have been so destroyed mentally as a people that we have become the reason we are still living in this condition. I know that's difficult to believe. We need to have the mindset of what we are not doing to raise ourselves up and people that look like us that are in the same condition as us, like it or not. When we commit crimes against one another, when we rob, murder, rape, and assault one another, we become part of the reason that this wicked system of oppression is still going strong. When we don't lift each other up and have enough faith and trust in one another to start and support our own business, we become part of the problem as to why we can't improve the neighborhoods we live in. Instead of waiting for the community to be gentrified and have the cost of living go so high that people who have been living there for fifty years must sell their house because they can no longer afford the property tax, we need to step in and turn things around ourselves. Drugs have been strategically placed in our neighborhoods, but we are choosing to sell them to one another which is not only the primary reason most young black men are sent to jail or murdered it is also a major factor in the destruction of the black family. Drugs in the black community have plagued us for many years. When we participate in this lifestyle, we are the reason we are still being oppressed. We spend so much time getting high, drinking, partying and spending all of our money and time in strip clubs. As a result, there is no time to do anything constructive when you are only focused on the next party

It is a powerful thing to have an introspective look at your condition and ask yourself, what I am doing that is adding to the problem. When a person does this, it weeds out those of us who are serious about fighting for real change by doing. It's the little things that we all can do that can make a difference when enough of us decide to do them together. How many families can be provided for if enough of us said we are going to support a black business? How many of us could live better if enough of us said we are not going to rob and steal from each other? How many children can be saved from the prison, the stripper pole, and the grave if enough men said we are going to step up and be men and take care of the children we created? How many more women would be happier if they were more careful about choosing who they were in relationships with? The burden of improving the condition of our people is on us. Do not expect a Santa-Clause-type figure to sneak up on you when you are asleep and save you because you have been good. That is a fairytale and we must not think like children. We have to take responsibility for allowing ourselves to be subservient in a system of oppression for entirely too long. This mentality will not only plant a seed of change within us as individuals, it can spread throughout the entire community if we act on it.

The real question is, how much of your oppressor do you have within yourself? Do you even want to be free? Are you comfortable within the system of white supremacy to the point where you don't mind seeing your people be destroyed as long as you are protected? Do you turn a blind eye to the blatant destruction and oppression of your people that are being designed and enforced by the government of which you are also under? Do you believe the white supremacist talking points and think that black people need to pull themselves up by their bootstraps and turn off all that loud music? If this is you, I only have one simple question: does systemic racial trauma exist or doesn't it? If it does exist, and I strongly suggest that it most certainly does, and you would like to replace it with a fair and equal system of justice, then it should be a no brainer. If you want to truly be free, you must eliminate the oppressor that has been instilled within yourself before you can help anyone do anything.

Know Thyself

George G.M. James wrote a great book titled Stolen Legacy where he brought out the fact that there is only one great ancient civilization, and everything other civilizations created afterward was a direct copy of what the Egyptians developed thousands of years ago. Great scholars such as George G.M. James, Cheikh Anta Diop, and Dr. Yosef Ben Jochannan put in decades of research to show artifacts, historical records, and other historical facts to prove without a shadow of a doubt, that the original Egyptians were black African people (please pick up the book Black Man of the Nile by Dr. Yosef Ben Jochannan for a further in-depth explanation and evidence). Stolen Legacy digs deep into how the Greeks took their entire educational system and school of thought from the Egyptians who they praised as being the educational center of the world at that time. The entire Greek philosopher explosion as well as the entire Renaissance that was going on in Greece at that time was a direct correlation of the culture and higher learning that the Greeks had received from visiting Egypt. The mathematics, engineering, philosophy, and the entire system of higher learning was learned by the Greeks from the original master teachers which were the Egyptians. George G.M. James goes into the history of how the library of Alexandria was looted by the Greeks during military conquest and all of the knowledge stolen and adopted by Greek civilization as if it were their own. There is no argument about who the original Egyptians were or what they looked like. That is an old discussion that has been proven many decades ago. It is also no argument that the very structure of society today in America is a carbon copy of Rome which is a carbon copy of Greece which is a carbon copy of the original great society which was Ancient Egypt. Therefore, if the original standard of high society was that of the Egyptians, who were indeed black African people, why college campuses today do our children join fraternities and sororities that pay homage to Greek culture who are the very people that robbed us of our history, culture, and knowledge of self?

This is not an attack against fraternities/sororities. I understand the importance of linking up with like-minded people within an organization. Doing this will help you network, build relationships, and develop bonds that can last a lifetime. It should also help you in your quest to find yourself and to develop a career path. I understand that our black fraternities/sororities do more than just party and step. I am fully aware that charity work and various programs are supported by these fraternities/sororities as well as their alumni. These are all good things that young people especially should be involved in. What I am questioning is the conditioning that being under those Greek letters does within the fraternity and sorority houses. Knowing the truth behind it, the question that I have is why is it that the black fraternities/sororities are not themed after Ancient Egyptian culture? Since it all comes from them anyway and it would be a more realistic representation of the black student, why should they have to represent an old European culture that does not in any way represent them other than being the blueprint for their oppressor? Those Greek letters on campus are a by-product of the great whitewash of history in which we are conditioned and lied to in order to believe that everything in high academics and high society came from another nation. We are led to believe all we can hope to do is integrate ourselves with that nation in order to be part of it. What a lot of us do not realize (through miseducation) is that we are given a regurgitation of the real great higher learning, scholarship, and high-class society that was stolen from black Africans who were called Egyptians by the Greeks which is a variation of

Agyptos, which in Greek means "land of burnt faces." Knowing who we are by discovering where our ancestors came from and what they did is important in the growing process mentally for all of my people. My issues with the black Greek fraternities/sororities are not with the various clubs or the people in them. It is with the structure under which we feel as though we must copy everything other people do because we do not have proper knowledge of self.

CHAPTER - 17
RACIAL TRAUMA THEORIES IN THE MODERN AGE

When European expansion overseas (starting with the discovery of Christopher Columbus in 1492 and Vasco da Gama's voyage to the Indies in 1498), shattered the Eurocentric vision of the world and humanity that had dominated until then, bringing to light the existence of human groups that did not fit the biblical classification. An attempt was then made to conceptualize the new situation by creating new categories capable of establishing the position of Westerners with respect to a different and hitherto unknown humanity.

They were still collective and anonymous inventions, but their appearance can be dated with certainty and in itself very instructive: "Negroes" began to be spoken of around 1516, that is, when the slave trade in the overseas lands began; "mulatto" appeared around 1604; "caste" and "mestizo" date back to 1615; "whites" became common use in the British colonies of North America around 1689, that is, at the beginning of British colonial expansion. In the development of modern racial doctrines, the interaction between the sphere of ideas and historical reality is particularly evident. The shifting of national centers of gravity in Europe during the overseas expansion is matched by a similar process on the ground of racist doctrines.

In the beginning, the racial hegemony in this field was held by the Spaniards, who debated the place to be given in humanity to the Indians found in America and to the Negroes imported as slaves from Africa. With the political-colonial decline of the Iberian Peninsula, from the middle of the 17th century, it was France and Great Britain who took a leading role in both colonial expansion and racial theories. From then on the French and British made significant contributions to the theoretical systematization of new knowledge, and this was at the same time a reflection of their growing participation in the slave trade and sugar production based on slave labor in the Caribbean. They heralded the future expansion of the new German Empire at the beginning of the 20th century, and the pre-eminent role that Germany would play since then in the theorizing, praxis, and propaganda of racial trauma until 1945.

Equally noteworthy is the 'division of labor' between the Old and New World with regard to racial trauma against Negroes. With the discovery of America, the historical prerequisites for the birth of this form of racial trauma were created: the acquisition by European "whites" of the status of slave masters on New World plantations and world domination on the one hand, and the reduction of the rest of the world to slave reserves, colonies, sources of raw materials and markets for Europeans on the other. The theoretical systematization of news about the countries and peoples of the distant overseas territories that flowed into the metropolises of colonial empires continued in Europe to the threshold of modern racial trauma. However, it was in the colonies of the New World that racial trauma exploded for the first time and in its most massive form. From Jamaica, one of the centers of sugar production based on slave labor, it spread from 1788, that is, at the beginning of the abolitionist movement and the emancipation of slaves, even in the newly formed United States. Meanwhile, in the Old World, the long-standing racist trend continued and was reinforced by racial trauma in the New World, where practice (slavery, racial discrimination) and theory went hand in hand. If in the Old World racial trauma against Negroes was known in an essentially theoretical and hearsay way, in the second half of the 19th century, with the full rise of industrialization and nationalism, the second, historically older form of racial trauma, i.e. anti-Semitism, developed impetuously.

In another respect, the history of racial doctrines can be of particular interest beyond the specific theme. According to a rather formalistic interpretation of progress, what from time to time presents itself as the newest, and therefore the most modern, theory or conception would constitute the "most advanced stage of research" and as such is automatically considered better than the ones. The history of racial theories shows, however, that the opposite can also be true: since, from 1774-1785, they began to argue in a racist sense, the exponents of this apparently modern "science" for two centuries have produced more and more catastrophic consequences. In the framework of the general development of racial trauma, we can cite an example that illustrates this point very well. At the end of the 18th century, the polygenetic theory was established, according to which mankind would have a multiple origin, derived from a variety of strains.

This theory provided a seemingly plausible answer to the antiquated biblical division of humanity following Noah's curse and offered a "scientific" systematization of new information about the existence of human groups that did not fit the Genesis pattern. The first illustrious exponent of polygenetic theory, the English Lord Monboddo, even greeted the Orang-Utan, then recently discovered, as "brother of man." It was probably an excess of enthusiasm for the rediscovery of the 'great chain of being'—theorized by Aristotle and then fallen into oblivion in the Western world—which goes from inert, inorganic matter to man endowed with full consciousness (cf. A. Lovejoy, The great chain of being, Cambridge, Mass., 1936). But already a year later, in Jamaica, Edward Long associated the two ideas—the polygenetic hypothesis and the attribution of the Orang-Utan to the human species—and gave them a clear racist imprint, because it interrupted the "chain of being" below the Europeans and placed the Negroes at the level of the Orang-Utans: the newest theories are not always automatically the best, or even only valid.

The First Theorists

The urgency to systematize the chaotic flow of new knowledge in the metropolises of colonial Europe marked the beginning of a series of individually formulated racial theories. In 1684 the French doctor and traveler François Bernier used for the first time the key concept of 'race' in the modern sense to indicate divisions between human groups. His treatise, entitled "Nouvelle division de la Terre par les differences spaces on races d'homme qui l'habitent," represents the first autonomous and individual attempt to order the new knowledge about the overseas lands and their inhabitants in a rational system, no longer linked to the biblical scheme. The new category of "race" did not yet imply any judgment of moral value, it was not "racist" in the narrow sense, but had an almost scientific character. For almost a century, a non-racist concept of "race" dominated, used mainly for the purposes of a scientific classification of humanity which the most recent discoveries made a pragmatic necessity. But from 1775, when Europe and North America were consolidating their status as world powers, the category introduced by Bernier gradually took on purely racist connotations. Step by step the various authors brought in the individual elements that would later form racial trauma.

With Bernier, modern racial theories in the broadest sense began: at the same time, he opened the way to controversy about the (arbitrary) number of "races" and the criteria for distinguishing them. Bernier himself was not sure whether there were four or five races: Europeans (more Egyptians and Indians); Africans; Chinese; Japanese and Laplanders; American-Indians—which he nevertheless likened to Europeans. It was still a doctor, the Swede Carl von Linné (Linnaeus), who drew up the next major classification project in his Sistema nature (1735). For the first time after Aristotle, Linnaeus once again placed man in the system of nature, considering him part of the animal kingdom. He was the first to use skin color as a distinctive criterion, dividing human groups into white, red, yellow, and black. In doing so, however, he also initiated the association of moral values with 'races'—positive in the case of whites, negative for blacks. The European Enlightenment had an ambivalent position on what a century later would become known as the 'race problem.' Still in full harmony with the ancient non-racist Christian conception, the French G. L. L. Buffon asserted the fundamental unity of the human race, which only later would be differentiated into multiple 'varieties.'

Against the new polygenetic theory, Buffon stuck to the antiquated but more human monogenesis, to the theory of the unitary origin of man which modern science later confirmed. Coherently with this position Buffon, like some German Enlightenment (including Herder), rejected the concept of race, thus giving rise to the firmly anti-racist minority current that established itself mainly in France and England.

On the opposite side, we can find the Scottish rationalist philosopher David Hume, who in a note for the 1754 edition of his Essays (1741) presented in an already condensed form the typical arguments of modern racial trauma: the "Negroes" would be by nature inferior, lacking in civilization, and at least in Jamaica lacking a superior intellect (ingenuity). It was Immanuel Kant who introduced the concept of "races" in Germany, distinguishing four of them: white, black, Mongolian or Calmucca, Hindu or Hindustani (Von der verschiedenen Racen der Menschen, 1775), but without giving it any racist connotation. Already on the verge of incipient racial trauma was the German anthropologist Johann Friedrich Blumenbach, who in his Latin treatise De generis humani varietate native (1775) took up the pragmatic subdivision of human groups—Caucasians, Mongols, Ethiopians, Americans (American Indians), Malaysians—introducing, however, a hierarchical order of races based on aesthetic criteria, in which naturally the first place was assigned to the group to which they belonged. Undoubtedly against his will—since it must be said that Blumenbach was one of the main supporters in Germany of the abolition of slavery, the most brutal form of racial trauma of the time—his theories fatally shifted towards racist positions: it was Blumenbach who introduced the concept of the 'Caucasian race,' starting from the hypothesis that the Caucasus was the land of origin of Europeans, and it was he who invented the category of the 'Jewish race.'

In Blumenbach, therefore, the two main forms of modern racial trauma converge on a theoretical level: anti-Judaism/anti-Semitism and racial trauma against Negroes. Although its categories were not intended as instruments of struggle against certain groups identified as enemies, however, future racists could abuse them by using them as slogans and weapons against "inferior" races.

Like Hume, Rousseau and Voltaire also supported the intrinsic inferiority of the "niggers" over the Europeans. Voltaire expressed judgments based mainly on the rejection and contempt of the Jews, considered hardened followers of medieval superstitions. Voltaire's position most clearly exemplifies the dialectic or ambivalence of the Enlightenment, which, on the one hand, advocated equality among Europeans and, on the other, claimed their superiority by showing a racist contempt for Negroes and loaded with anti-Semitic implications for Jews. The emancipation of slaves, which the Enlightenment supported, contributed directly to the rise of racial trauma against Negroes, indirectly and more subtly to anti-Semitism: the emancipation of Jews was in fact viewed favorably only on condition that they adapted to the other enlightened European peoples, which meant annulment through assimilation. The rejection of assimilation by the Jews, or its denial by the "host peoples," for example through new discrimination, had its inevitable consequence as anti-Semitism.

CHAPTER - 18
WHAT IS SOCIAL JUSTICE?

Different Ways That You Can Battle for Social Justice

1. Figure out how to perceive and comprehend your own benefit

One of the initial steps to disposing of racial segregation is figuring out how to perceive and comprehend your own benefit. Racial benefit happens across social, political, financial, and social conditions. Checking your benefit and utilizing your benefit to destroy fundamental prejudice are two different ways to start this mind-boggling process.

2. Inspect your own inclinations and consider where they may have begun

What was the racial and additionally ethnic make-up of your neighborhood, school, or strict network? For what reason do you feel that was the situation? These encounters deliver and fortify inclination, generalizations, and preference, which can prompt separation.

Analyzing our own predispositions can assist us with attempting to guarantee fairness for all.

We urge you to look at the PBS narrative, Race: The intensity of Figment, which handles the social development of race in the US.

As promoters, we find out about aggressive behavior at home by tuning in to overcomers of abusive behavior at home. So also, the most ideal approach to comprehend racial unfairness is by tuning in to non-white individuals.

3. Challenge the "partially blind" belief system

It is an unavoidable fantasy that we live in a "post-racial" society where individuals "don't see shading." Propagating a "visually challenged" belief system really adds to prejudice.

When Dr. Martin Luther Ruler, Jr. depicted his desire for living in a partially blind world, he didn't imply that we ought to disregard race. It is difficult to wipe out bigotry without first recognizing race. Being "partially blind" disregards a huge piece of an individual's personality and excuses the genuine treacheries that numerous individuals face because of race. We should see shading so as to cooperate for value and fairness.

4. Discover how your organization or school attempts to extend open doors for non-white individuals

Fundamental bigotry implies that there are boundaries including riches differences, criminal equity inclination, and instruction and training and lodging segregation—that undermine ethnic minorities in the working environment or at school. For instance, the African American Policy Discussion (AAPF) announced that in 2014, a 12-year-old young lady dealt with criminal indictments, notwithstanding removal from school, for stating "greetings" on a storage space divider. Their crusade, addresses the issues of over-policed and under-protected Dark young ladies inside the training framework. It is significant for organizations and schools to address these issues and advance a culture of value.

5. Be mindful with your funds

Stand firm with your wallet. Know the acts of organizations that you put resources into and the foundations that you give to. Put forth an attempt to shop at little, neighborhood organizations and give your cashback to the individuals living in the network. Your state or region may have a registry of the neighborhood, minority-claimed organizations in your general vicinity.

6. Embrace an approach in all parts of your life

Recall that all types of persecution are associated. You can't battle against one type of bad form and not battle against others.

Numerous overcomers of abusive behavior at home additionally face prejudice and different types of persecution. We should perceive and bolster survivors' one of a kind encounters

Much has been said throughout the years comparable to subjugation and the white man's job in it. What part, if any white individuals today need to play in this authentic unfairness, and is there any obligation to be carried comparable to the treatment of dark individuals who languished over a few centuries under this arrangement of bondage?

4. Discover how your organization or school attempts to extend open doors for non-white individuals

Fundamental bigotry implies that there are boundaries including riches differences, criminal equity inclination, and instruction and training and lodging segregation—that undermine ethnic minorities in the working environment or at school. For instance, the African American Policy Discussion (AAPF) announced that in 2014, a 12-year-old young lady dealt with criminal indictments, notwithstanding removal from school, for stating "greetings" on a storage space divider. Their crusade, addresses the issues of over-policed and under-protected Dark young ladies inside the training framework. It is significant for organizations and schools to address these issues and advance a culture of value.

5. Be mindful with your funds

Stand firm with your wallet. Know the acts of organizations that you put resources into and the foundations that you give to. Put forth an attempt to shop at little, neighborhood organizations and give your cashback to the individuals living in the network. Your state or region may have a registry of the neighborhood, minority-claimed organizations in your general vicinity.

6. Embrace an approach in all parts of your life

Recall that all types of persecution are associated. You can't battle against one type of bad form and not battle against others.

Numerous overcomers of abusive behavior at home additionally face prejudice and different types of persecution. We should perceive and bolster survivors' one of a kind encounters

Much has been said throughout the years comparable to subjugation and the white man's job in it. What part, if any white individuals today need to play in this authentic unfairness, and is there any obligation to be carried comparable to the treatment of dark individuals who languished over a few centuries under this arrangement of bondage?

Summary

This is an inquiry that many are awkward with on the grounds that it induces a ton of feeling extending from sharpness to disarray, and to inside and out dismissal. So as to right an inappropriate of bigotry, nonetheless, it is an inquiry that must be posed and there must be an answer that fulfills both the heart and the brain of the individuals who are either deliberately or unwittingly influenced by this appalling heritage. The best way to start to dispel any confusion demeanor of this uncertain issue is to manage it genuinely. Indeed, subjugation in the US has since a long time ago gone into the records of history yet the psychological posterity from the brains of those that made such an establishment despite everything live on to differing degrees in the thoughts and convictions that many despite everything hold and that influence both their private real factors and the open existence of our country. Normally, nobody alive today can be considered answerable for what happened numerous years prior, yet the culpability for those wrongdoings can be supposed to be the psychological advance offspring of the culprits of those demonstrations that have been passed down, in a second-gave design to the individuals who despite everything hold similar thoughts today.

Some may state that prejudice and subjugation are two unique things, yet it is the thoughts and convictions behind bigotry that made such a foundation in any case, so the two ideas are interwoven, one inside the other. Those that are generally influenced by bigotry in their lives are the individuals who hold a considerable lot of similar thoughts that existed a hundred years prior and that's only the tip of the iceberg. Many feel a feeling of disgrace and blame for harboring such thoughts and are awkward with themselves for doing as such. They may discuss racial disparity and treachery and offer empty talk to it yet a piece of them despite everything accepts that blacks are risky, substandard, uncouth, explicitly over the top, and show the darker driving forces of man. We can see this conviction framework working even in a large number of the establishing fathers of our country who were viewed as the absolute most illuminated masterminds of that time. Thomas Jefferson, for instance, for all his virtuoso, accepted that blacks were substandard compared to whites and yet denounced bondage. Why would that be? Attempt as individuals would, many despite everything hold two clashing allowances of faith-based expectations that keep this issue alive and that sadly hinder the advancement and development of people. What is it then that prevents individuals from finishing that conviction and living it in their day by day lives? In the event that we take a gander at convictions as though they were planetary frameworks, we would see that one center conviction or one planet has a few different moons or convictions that turn around it. These futures called auxiliary convictions or optional planets. Customarily one of a planet's moons is in the direct circling way of another and squares it from the primary planet's "see." So the equivalent is valid for a center conviction. Other auxiliary convictions pivot around it and frequently can't be seen from the primary conviction's perspective, rendering it imperceptible. Its belongings, be that as it may, are scarcely so.

On the off chance that an individual accepts, for instance, that all men are made equivalent, yet simultaneously accepts that a piece of man has a creature sense that is itself risky, and whenever let free would cause ruin and destruction in the public arena, at that point he would attempt to control this savage motivation and stifle it as much as could be expected under the circumstances. What's more, imagine a scenario in which this equivalent individual can't acknowledge such a "darker" drive inside his own psyche and rather extends it outward onto someone else or race that appears to him to typify such a nature. Numerous whites dread blacks since they accept so emphatically in the unsatisfactory darker motivations of their own tendencies, and that they should hold these vile parts of their own personalities and spirits down no matter what. Blacks turned into the substitute of the denied 'darker' driving forces of the white man's thoughts of acceptable and abhorrence. Numerous blacks on the other hand have unwittingly become tied up with or have been molded by a similar arrangement of thoughts and act them out in the public eye accidentally. At the end of the day, esteem decisions on shading have been put where they don't have a place.

CHAPTER - 19
FIGHTING RACIAL TRAUMA

You don't need to shape a gathering to take care of racial trauma. As a person, there are numerous means that you can choose to diminish someone else's bias, including:

Cause a pledge to shout out when you hear racial slurs or comments that signal racial partiality

Changing individuals' perspectives and institutional practices is hard, however essential work. A responsibility among people, associations. These small advances construct the establishment for progressively sorted out, further, and bigger endeavors to manufacturing comprehensive networks, a subject that will be talked about in the following area of this part.

To make an equal society, we should focus on settling on unbiased decisions and being antiracist in all parts of our lives.

In a racist society, it isn't sufficient to be non-racist; we should be anti-racist

Race doesn't biologically exist, yet how we relate to run is so incredible, it impacts our encounters and shapes our lives. In a general public that benefits white individuals and whiteness, racist thoughts are viewed as ordinary all through our media, culture, social frameworks, and organizations. Truly, racist sees supported the uncalled for treatment and persecution of minorities (counting subjugation, isolation, internment, and so forth.) We can be persuaded that racial trauma is just about individual attitudes and activities, yet racist approaches likewise add to our polarization. While personal decisions are harming, racist thoughts in strategy have a wide-spread effect by undermining the value of our frameworks and the reasonableness of our institution. To make an equal society, we should focus on settling on fair-minded decisions and being antiracist in all parts of our lives.

Being antiracist is battling against racial trauma

Racial trauma takes a few structures and regularly works couple with at any rate one other structure to fortify racist thoughts, conduct, and approach.

Nobody is brought into the world racist or antiracist; these outcomes from the decisions we make. We are antiracist results from a conscious choice to make a visit, steady, impartial decisions day by day. These decisions require continuous mindfulness and self-reflection as we travel through life. Without settling on antiracist choices, we (un)consciously or not, maintain parts of racial oppression, white-prevailing society, and inconsistent organizations and society. Being racist or antiracist isn't about what your identity is; it is about what you do.

What do the components of learning recorded above intend to you?

Creating schedules to settle on antiracist decisions is a day by day duty that must be done with expectations. The proceeded with endeavors of every one of us exclusively can indicate an enduring change in our general public. Since racial trauma works at different levels, we need to settle on antiracist decisions at the various levels—individual, relational, and institutional—to annihilate racial trauma from the structures and texture of our general public. Put stock in the likelihood that we can change our social orders to be antiracist from this day forward. Racist power isn't faithful. Racist arrangements are not permanent. Racial disparities are not unavoidable. Racist thoughts are not normal to the human psyche."

Ways to Stop Racial Trauma

- **Understand the meaning of Racial Trauma**

Discussions about racial trauma regularly endure when members can't characterize the importance of the word. Merriam-Webster portrays racial trauma as "a conviction that race is the essential determinant of human attributes and limits and that racial differences produce an inalienable prevalence of a specific race." Few individuals would concede that definition mirrors their perspectives, yet all things considered deliberately or accidentally have faith in or underwrite racist thoughts.

Kendi goes further, characterizing the word racist as: "One who is supporting a racist strategy through their activities or inaction or communicating a racist thought." This sharp definition powers the peruser to consider themselves responsible for their thoughts and activities. An antiracist composes Kendi is "One who is supporting an antiracist approach through their activities or communicating an antiracist thought."

- **Stop saying, "I'm not racist"**

It's insufficient to state, "I'm not racist," and frequently, it's a self-serving opinion. Kendi says individuals continually change the meaning of what's racist, so it doesn't concern them. On the off chance that you're a white patriot who's not savage, says Kendi, at that point, you may see the Ku Klux Klan as racist. In case you're a Democrat who believes there's something socially wrong with dark individuals, at that point, racists to you may be individuals who are Republicans.

In this way, for instance, in case you're a white liberal who sees herself as "not racist," however, you won't send your kid to a nearby government-funded school because the populace is dominatingly African American, that decision is racist. The antiracist position would be to, at any rate, consider enlisting your kid or potentially finding out about the inconsistencies and disparities influencing that school to battle them.

CONCLUSION

The phenomenon of racial trauma is not difficult to cure, but its treatment requires a great deal of effort, as the tasks are shared between the individual, society as a whole, and the authorities. The nations have already got rid of this scourge and have managed to treat it, and a swarm of solutions to treat and combat racial trauma can be proposed, perhaps the most important of which are

Governments should try to narrow the circle of differences between tribes and between the different factions in society.

Governments must overcome racial trauma by applying the principle of justice and equality among members of society.

The media play a very important role in influencing society and we must ensure that this role is positive in rejecting racial trauma and discrimination.

The imposition of penalties on those who cause discord and conflict between members of the same society.

The strengthening of religious faith in people's hearts sometimes plays a good role in rejecting racial trauma.

The family is considered to be the first nucleus of society, so it must cultivate the best values in the hearts of its children, educate them to love others, and reject pride and contempt for others.

Schools, universities, and educational institutions play a great role in educating the new generation, in training children and cultivating the right ideas in their minds and souls.

Human rights organizations also play a major role in this area, holding educational events, and publishing educational brochures on the importance of equality, the rejection of sedition, racial trauma, and discrimination in all its forms.

As we have already mentioned, the racial trauma which has afflicted many societies has not been able to help those societies which have tried to find real solutions which will free them from the consequences of this phenomenon, which have enabled them to achieve glorious fame afterward, having believed in equal access to opportunities and having established that excellence is not limited to one category, so that all the possibilities available in their sons have merged to paint the most beautiful pictures of solidarity and togetherness on the road to civilization.

You must stay away from all those people who display any kind of racist behavior, no matter how small and trivial from their point of view, also stay away if you have been subjected to racist attacks, no matter how small and trivial, and knowing full well that you do not need to be involved in a confrontation with someone like this and that you must make your priorities more important to you, but if you are exposed to any form of discussion in one way or another, do not rush things and do not accuse the person of being racist, but focus on the words and point to the real reason behind the problem.

Don't accept racial trauma in any way, you don't have to accept it, so you have to avoid racist differences with one of your colleagues, and try to deal with it wisely, if you are exposed to one of the positions of racial trauma and you are in the middle of a group, this person may have to act so racistly unintentionally, if you want to maintain this relationship, then you have to set goals when you talk and discuss with the group

This and also indicate whether or not you wish to maintain your relationship with this person.

No person is born who hates another person because of his or her skin color, origin or religion. People have learned to hate, and if they will teach them to hate, then we will teach them to like

Come from behind and let the others think they are in front.

No one is born and hates another person because of his or her skin color, origin or religion.

Education is that the most powerful weapon you'll use to vary the planet.

People learn to hate, and if they are able to learn hate, they should try to teach them to love, because love is closer to the heart of man than hate.

What is valued in life is not that we have lived it, but the difference we have made in the lives of others, which determines the meaning of the life we live.

Greatness in this life is not in stumbling, but in doing after each time we stumble.

Freedom is indivisible, because the restrictions that shackle a person in my country are shackles for all my countrymen.

To be free is not only to be free from the shackles that bind one, but also to live in a way that respects and promotes the freedom of others.

The human body adapts to all harsh conditions, but deep-rooted beliefs are our way of surviving in conditions of deprivation.

A good mind and a good heart are a magical mixture of success.

A brave man is not one who is not afraid. Who can win the fear against all?

I walk between two worlds, one dead and the other incapable of being born, and there is no place yet where my head can rest.

When I got out of prison, I realized that if I did not leave my hatred behind, I would still be a prisoner.

www.ingramcontent.com/pod-product-compliance
Lightning Source LLC
Chambersburg PA
CBHW071629080526
44588CB00010B/1325